Normal Bad Boys

Main building, The Boys' Farm and Training School, Shawbridge, Quebec, circa 1909.

Normal Bad Boys

Public Policies, Institutions, and the Politics of Client Recruitment

PRUE RAINS AND ELI TERAM

McGill-Queen's University Press
Montreal & Kingston • London • Buffalo

© McGill-Queen's University Press 1992
ISBN 0-7735-0906-2

Legal deposit fourth quarter 1992
Bibliothèque nationale du Québec

Printed in Canada on acid-free paper

This book has been published with the help of a grant
from the Social Science Federation of Canada, using
funds provided by the Social Sciences and Humanities
Research Council of Canada.

Canadian Cataloguing in Publication Data

Rains, Prue
  Normal bad boys
  Includes bibliographical references and index.
  ISBN 0-7735-0906-2

  1. Juvenile corrections – Quebec (Province). 2. Juvenile
  delinquents – Rehabilitation – Quebec (Province).
  3. Juvenile justice, Administration of – Quebec
  (Province). 4. Shawbridge Youth Centres.
  I. Teram, Eli, 1949–   . II. Title.

  HV9110.M65R35 1992   364.3'6'09714   C92-090236-7

Portions, revisions, and translations of the following articles have been reprinted
with permission from: Society for the Study of Social Problems: Rains, P., 1984,
"Juvenile Justice and The Boys' Farm: Surviving a Court-Created Population Crisis,
1909–1948," *Social Problems* 31: 500–13; Presses de l'Université de Montréal: Rains, P.,
1985, "La justice des mineurs et The Boys' Farm: 1909–1968," *Criminologie* XVIII (1):
103–27; Canadian Association of Schools of Social Work: Teram, E., 1988, "The
Politics of Interorganizational Structures," *Canadian Social Work Review* 5: 236–51;
Children and Youth Service Review: Teram, E., 1988, "From Self-managed Hearts to
Collective Action: Dealing with Incompatible Demands in the Child Welfare
System," *Children and Youth Services Review* 10: 305–15; Teram, E. and G. Erickson,
1988, "The Protection of Children's Rights as Ceremony and Myth: A Critique of the
Review of Institutional Placements in Quebec and Ontario," *Children and Youth
Services Review* 10: 1–17; Sage Publications: Rains, P. and E. Teram, 1991, "The
Transformation of Strategies for Controlling Admissions: Professionalization and
Youth Processing Organizations," *Crime and Delinquency* 37 (2): 281–99.

Typeset in Palatino 10/12 by Caractéra production graphique inc., Quebec City.

To Bluma Teram

To Adam Rains,
    Matt and Michelle Fortier

Contents

Acknowledgments

At the outset, we would both like to thank Shawbridge Youth Centres, the Ville Marie Social Services Centre, Youth Horizons and the Youth Horizons Foundation, the Jewish Family Services Social Services Centre, and the Anglophone Advisory Committee for the remarkable "inside" access to the past and present provided to us. Their openness to serious inquiry has made this study possible. For the historical study, we acknowledge particularly the support received from Joe Borgo, Doug Brice, and Rhea Seath. As for the contemporary study, our special thanks go to the workers and managers who allowed access to their meetings and answered the many questions.

Many scholars made truly helpful comments on numerous earlier versions of this manuscript: Frank McGilly, David Woodsworth, Malcolm Spector, Howard Becker, Hal Benenson, Michael Smith, James Hackler, Carol Warren, John Kitsuse, Joan Stelling, Cathy Watson, Jack Rains, and James Lewis.

We received funding to support portions of this project from Montreal's Allied Jewish Community Services, the Max Bell Fund, the Government of Quebec (FCAC and CQRS), Shawbridge Youth Centres, and Canada Manpower. At McGill University, support came from the Faculty of Graduate Studies and Research, the Faculty of Arts and the Sociology Department, and the School of Social Work. At the University of Windsor, the Research Grants Committee provided funding. At Wilfrid Laurier University, support came from the Research Grants Committee and the Academic Development Fund.

Cadet corps, The Boys' Farm and Training School, Shawbridge, Quebec, circa 1915.

Normal Bad Boys

CHAPTER ONE

Social Policies
and Institutions
for Problem Youth

This study traces the history of public policies affecting the disposition of delinquent, neglected, and emotionally disturbed anglophone youth in Montreal. We have examined the impact of these policies on youth-processing organizations and their clients from the vantage point of a single organization – one that, over the course of its long history, has been variously linked to other organizations in Montreal's delinquency, child-welfare, and mental health networks. Our analysis of this history, and of the active part The Boys' Farm played both in shaping the impact of new policies and in controlling admissions, addresses the many explanations put forth concerning the unintended effects of similar public policies elsewhere in Canada and the United States.

The Boys' Farm and Training School was founded in 1908 in Shawbridge, forty miles northwest of Montreal, by a group of philanthropic Protestant Montreal businessmen. Based on the country "cottage model," it was intended as a nonprison setting for the reformation of Protestant delinquent boys through outdoor work and living. It was the Province of Quebec's only reform school for non-Catholic, non-French-speaking delinquent boys, including the children of immigrants who, as Rothman (1971) noted, came to populate reform schools during times of high immigration. Most boys came from the Montreal area.

The Boys' Farm, now known as Shawbridge Youth Centres, operates as a major "reception centre" in Montreal's provincially regulated, anglophone child-welfare network. Today, Shawbridge provides differential-treatment programs for more than 200 delinquent boys and girls from the ages of fourteen to eighteen. Its residential services include locked, fenced, or highly structured security units and less structured cottages at its original country site, as well as community group homes in Montreal.

Beneath the apparent continuity of its mandate to deal with Montreal's anglophone delinquents, the eighty-year history of The Boys' Farm (1908–88) spans major shifts of public policy affecting the disposition and institutional placement of delinquent, neglected, and emotionally disturbed youth. These public policies and their effects have become the object of critical sociological, historical, and criminological attention. Interest has focused particularly on the invention of the juvenile court, the "net-widening" impact of juvenile justice reforms,[1] and the phenomenon known as "transcarceration."[2]

REFORMS AND
THE CRITICAL VIEW

The juvenile justice movement – its views reflected in Canada by the passage of the Juvenile Delinquents Act (1908) – not only promoted separate court and detention facilities for youth, as well as a welfare-oriented concern with the situation and "best interests" of the child, but also pushed for practices designed to mitigate and individualize justice. For example, the movement advocated the use of probation to keep delinquents out of institutions, and indefinite sentences tailored to improvements in behaviour. Later reforms provided new alternatives to the reform school: psychiatrists and social workers, attached to juvenile-court clinics, referred youth to family-counselling services, while group-home and day programs provided community-based residential and nonresidential alternatives. More recently, policies have been designed to reduce and prohibit the incarceration of status offenders.[3] Most recently, a wide variety of so-called diversion programs have promoted additional alternatives, not just to incarceration but also to contacts with the juvenile court itself. These juvenile-justice reforms – usually sponsoring the view that children, even delinquent ones, belong in families rather than institutions – have been promoted as benevolent and progressive reforms for youth.

Revisionist interpretations of the early juvenile-justice movement challenged the benevolent intent of the juvenile-justice reformers; these interpretations emphasized the expansionist and essentially coercive impact of the juvenile court as a form of state intervention into the lives of working-class children and their families. Platt (1969), for example, observes that the first American juvenile court in Chicago actually increased reform-school populations. The revisionist view has, in turn, been challenged, or qualified, by those who find it incompatible with the ideas held by juvenile-justice reformers

(Mennel 1973, 1983); the lack of a direct connection to ruling-class interests (Hagan and Leon 1977); or the alternative evidence that the new juvenile courts might, in fact, not have increased reform-school populations (Schlossman 1977; Hagan and Leon 1977). In their study of the first Canadian juvenile court in Toronto (1912), Hagan and Leon (1977) argue that that court emphasized probation and reduced incarceration;[4] they contend that, unlike the United States, the Canadian legislation and context emphasized probation as an "informal" rather than a "criminalizing" means of social control.

Critical attention to later juvenile-justice reforms centred on the unintended net-widening effects of these innovations. Researchers focused, in other words, on how policies designed to provide substitutes for incarceration and formal adjudication instead supplemented and widened the net of social control, drawing more youths into new programs while preserving and filling the old institutions.[5] Although most studies examined policies affecting the disposition of delinquents, recent findings draw attention to the interpenetration of the three youth-processing networks dealing with problem youths (the delinquency, child-welfare, and mental health networks). For instance, in 1974, American legislation, designed to encourage the decarceration of status offenders from reform schools, instead produced "transinstitutionalization" (Warren 1981); that is, the transfer of status offenders from reform schools to public and private psychiatric hospitals (Lerman 1982; Warren and Guttridge 1984). Indeed, in 1977, when California legislation *required* the removal of all status offenders from locked institutions (reform schools and juvenile-court detention centres), status offenders were then relabelled as "delinquent," "neglected," or "emotionally disturbed" youths, thus justifying their placement in locked institutions in all three youth-processing networks (Van Dusen 1981).

These discoveries suggest that studies that focus exclusively on the disposition of delinquent, neglected, or emotionally disturbed youth inadvertently reify the very concepts they are, often implicitly, calling into question. Distinctions among delinquency, neglect, and emotional disturbance classifications, for example, have often reflected the orientations of those who impose them. As Rothman (1980, 229) noted, "In practice the distinction between the neglected and the delinquent child often depended less upon what the child had done than upon the credentials of the complaining officer. If a policeman intervened, the child came up on delinquency; if a representative of a child-care agency acted, the child came up on neglect." In fact, the characteristics that distinguish delinquent, neglected, and emotionally disturbed youths from one another (or from "normal" youths more generally) may only seem obvious once labelling has occurred. Clearly, the processes through which problem youths become so defined are, themselves, empirical matters worthy of both contemporary and historical exploration.

The concept of transcarceration in effect widens the viewing frame with which we examine the history of policies affecting the disposition of delinquents – to include those policies affecting the disposition of neglected and emotionally disturbed youth. The modern child-welfare network has its origins in the children's aid societies' campaigns to place neglected children in adoptive or foster homes rather than orphanages. Thus the expansion of foster-home placement, accelerated by the emergence of welfare support for poor families, radically reduced orphanage populations, putting many out of business (Lerman 1982, 107–23; Rooke and Schnell 1983, 273–329). Social service agencies were faced, however, with limits on both the supply of foster homes and the selectivity of foster parents (their preference being young and normal children). Older and more disturbed youths were therefore referred to "respecialized" children's institutions,[6] or to newly emerging children's psychiatric services and institutions in the mental health network (Lerman 1982, 107–50). Nevertheless, in his 1982 evaluation of the decarceration movement in the United States, Lerman concludes that the successful decarceration of neglected youths was offset by the new incarceration of emotionally disturbed youths, and that the rates of youth incarceration had actually increased.[7]

*Understanding the Unintended Impact
of Public Policies*

Net-widening and transcarceration can be explained in several overlapping ways. One implicit, but often ambiguous, explanation has involved framing the issue in terms of expanded social and state control. Indeed, net-widening studies usually rely on the stated purposes of new public policies to argue that the latter's unintended consequences should be viewed negatively – that is, as expanded social control rather than as, say, expanded service.[8] Although this interpretation is persuasive, it renders ambiguous an implicit claim about the role of the state in expanding social control: that is, were the new policies actually intended to expand state control, or not?

A second explanation focuses on the relevance of new funding arrangements in altering the patterns of institutional use – again whether intended or not. Lerman (1982) argues, for example, that, in the United States after 1961, federal financial support for placements in private or medical institutions vastly expanded the use of private institutions for troubled youth. Warren and Guttridge (1984) argue that increases in private medical insurance facilitated both the placement of troubled youth in private psychiatric facilities and the increased "medicalization" of their troubles. More general political-economy explanations emphasize the growth, and later the economic crisis, of the welfare state, as well as the discovery of low-cost control mechanisms, and the ensuing "commodification" of "social junk" (Scull 1977) through the state's transfer of its responsibility for social misfits to the profit-oriented private sector.

A third explanation emphasizes the role that organizations play in subverting new policies; that is, that by putting them to "convenient" use, they, at times, produce unintended effects (Rothman 1980). This explanation draws attention to those organizational interests affecting the disposition of clients so often documented in studies of human-service organizations. Take, for example, the organizations' preference for "overqualified" clients,[9] as well as their development of devices to ward off undesirable clients (Lang 1981), not to mention their simultaneous attempts to recruit, select, and hold on to "good clients" (Scott 1967a,b; Peyrot 1982). The interorganizational transactions that may be involved in referring or transferring clients from one organization to another are clearly an arena for client-recruitment politics. Witness the many strategies devised by such organizations to help themselves recruit, select, exclude, and weed out clients, in the face of their involvement with one another as the suppliers and receivers of clients.

In the disposition of delinquent, neglected, and emotionally disturbed youth, the juvenile court has served as a central organizational link for the transfer of clients within and across youth-processing networks. Thus, the child-welfare network has relied on the juvenile court to transfer the neglected youth it cannot place (its "dead-endies") to reform schools (Emerson 1969). The juvenile court, in turn, has relied on the mental health network to provide clinical assessment services, recommendations regarding case disposition, and contacts that facilitate the transfer of delinquents to psychiatric institutions (Emerson 1969; Hatch 1987; Warren and Guttridge 1984). The authority of the juvenile court to distribute clients is limited, however, to publicly contracted institutions.

A fourth explanation focuses on the expansion of the role of treatment-oriented professionals (psychiatrists, clinical psychologists, and social workers). Not only have these professionals played a part in creating new domains for their services, they have also used the language of treatment to both shape and justify their disposition of clients (Lerman 1982; Cohen 1985). The clinical orientation of professionals mutes distinctions among delinquent, neglected, and emotionally disturbed youth through the use of such concepts as "conduct disorders" and "acting out," thus encouraging flexible, appropriate responses to young clients and their troubles. However, that same flexibility can respond to the needs and interests of youth-processing organizations by permitting them to define clients in ways that are organizationally convenient rather than clinically appropriate.

PUBLIC POLICIES AND THE BOYS' FARM

Juvenile Justice and The Boys' Farm

During its early history (1908–50), The Boys' Farm was directly affected by the "invention" of the juvenile court. Indeed, Quebec's first provincial juvenile court, established in Montreal in 1912, flourished until 1940 as the province's only juvenile court, supplying clients to all four of Montreal's private reform schools.[10] All four reform schools were affected by the court's policies.

Like Montreal's other private reform schools, The Boys' Farm contracted with the provincial government to receive court-committed clients, in exchange for a per diem subsidy for each court-committed boy. Reform schools supplemented these subsidies with charitable donations and, in the case of the Catholic institutions, with workers supplied by religious orders. As an English Protestant charity, The Boys' Farm benefited from the charitable involvements and sense of mission of the wealthy and influential Montreal businessmen who served on its board of directors. In fact, until the late 1960s, the province did not play an active part in regulating the private institutions it funded. This long absence of public control, due in large measure to provincial deference to the autonomy of private Catholic institutions, distinguishes the history of the Province of Quebec's institutional support from that of the other provinces in Canada, as well as from that of the United States.

The early history of The Boys' Farm provides new evidence as to the immediate impact of the juvenile court on Canadian reform-school populations, while situating, somewhat, the activism of prominent businessmen on behalf of juvenile-justice reforms. But the invention of the juvenile court had a more profound and lasting effect: it established a new interorganizational context within which the juvenile court could control the access of reform schools to clients.

To date, little attention has been paid to the relations between juvenile courts and reform schools regarding the disposition of clients, to the effects of new court policies on the size and composition of reform-school populations over time, or to the efforts of reform schools to control the disposition of clients. Our analysis will show that juvenile-court policies have intermittently threatened reform-school populations more seriously than the revisionist view has suggested.[11] We will also show how and why The Boys' Farm attempted to use its resources as a private institution to control both the disposition of clients and the impact of the court.

In the first section of this book, we examine the politics of client recruitment within the interorganizational context created by the invention of the juvenile court. In the introduction, we look at Montreal's reform schools prior to the passage of Canada's Juvenile Delinquents Act (1908), the key features of the subsequent new legislation, and the Province of Quebec's first juvenile court in Montreal. Chapter 2 focuses on the efforts of The Boys' Farm to control the size of its client population in the face of juvenile-court policies that threatened its client population and budget. Chapter 3 examines the reform school's lengthy efforts to control the composition of its client population in the face of the juvenile court's increased use of the reform school as a last resort for older, delinquent recidivists.

Youth Protection and The Boys' Farm

In 1950, with the new provincial child-welfare legislation, The Boys' Farm became not just a reform school for delinquents, but also a "youth-protection school" for neglected youth. As such, the reform school remained dependent on the juvenile court for clients of both kinds; however, it now had to compete for desirable "protection" clients with Montreal's other child-welfare and emerging mental health institutions.

The ensuing disposition of neglected and emotionally disturbed youth reflected the degree of organizational control over admissions exercised by the private youth-processing organizations. It also reflected the organizations' efforts to retain historical claims over certain kinds of clients, as well as the juvenile court's failure to acquire control over the disposition of clients in the private child-welfare and mental health networks. As a result, the juvenile court and publicly contracted youth-protection schools, such as The Boys' Farm, were compelled to handle the "dead-endies" from the child-welfare and mental health networks. After 1950, The Boys' Farm was therefore affected by developments within a wider interorganizational context than before; that new breadth altered not only the composition of its client population but also its strategies for controlling admissions.

In the mid-1960s, both the new Quebec nationalism and certain federal policies began to alter the organizational environment within which all of the province's private social-welfare organizations were operating. These broader political and economic developments generated explicit interorganizational activity within Montreal's anglophone social-welfare network. They also provided The Boys' Farm with opportunities for realignment with the child-welfare network, and, by shifting authority to the child-welfare network, further eroded the authority of Montreal's juvenile court over the disposition of neglected, emotionally disturbed, and delinquent youths.

The second section of this book examines the politics of client recruitment within the wider interorganizational context created by The Boys' Farm's new status, after 1950, as a youth-protection school. By focusing on policies affecting the disposition of neglected rather than delinquent youths, this second section retraces the period from 1950 to 1966 from a different vantage point. Its introduction steps even further back, setting Montreal's child-welfare institutions and provincial child-welfare policies within an historical context. Chapter 4, while showing how client-disposition practices in the child-welfare and mental health networks were responsible for sending more and more seriously emotionally disturbed "protection" clients to The Boys' Farm, documents the strategies used by that institution to manage and control the disposition of these clients. But, although these strategies were still linked largely to the juvenile court, they began to include new contacts with mental health and child-welfare organizations. Chapter 5 looks at the growing threat of provincial intervention, its impact on interorganizational relations within Montreal's anglophone child-welfare network, and the strategies used by The Boys' Farm both to realign its position in the child-welfare network and to acquire control over admissions. These strategies successfully exploited the advice of professional experts, thereby permitting The Boys' Farm to gain access to newly available public funds.

A Mandated Youth-in-Trouble Network

In 1971, sweeping provincial legislation reorganized the entire Quebec social and health-services sector into formal regional groupings under public control. The reorganized child-welfare network not only grouped social service agencies into regional "social service centres," but also redefined child-welfare institutions as regional "reception centres." One of the largest social service centres was formed by amalgamating Montreal's anglophone social service agencies; at the same time, Montreal's anglophone child-welfare institutions – including The Boys' Farm – became reception centres in the same regional network.

In 1977, the Quebec Youth Protection Act vastly expanded the authority of the reorganized child-welfare network: delinquents as well as neglected youth were now sent to "directors of youth protection" in social service centres, rather than to juvenile courts, for their initial assessment and disposition. The Province of Quebec thus installed a model child-welfare system designed to keep most young people from stigmatizing contact with the juvenile court. Institutional placement decisions were now made by "joint admissions committees," that included representatives from both social service and reception centres.

The third section of this book examines the politics of client recruitment in Montreal's anglophone youth-protection network – the second largest such network in the Province of Quebec, and a major Canadian youth-in-trouble network. In this new interorganizational context, reception centres acquired surprising control over the disposition of clients, thus subverting the intention of public policy to allocate this control to social service centres. Even more suprisingly, the anglophone social service centre failed to use its authority to dispose of clients, thus sacrificing the professional autonomy of its social workers as well as the external review procedures designed to protect children's rights. An introduction to this section outlines the integration of the child-welfare and juvenile delinquency systems. Chapters 6 and 7 then document the interests and strategies that affected the disposition of clients, by examining the changing structure of the joint-admissions committee, and the negotiations that redefined clients on a case-by-case basis to fit the organizational needs and interests of reception centres. Chapter 8 shows how the procedures for external review, designed to protect children's rights, were watered down in ways that gave reception centres largely unrestricted control over the treatment of their clients.

THE ARGUMENT: OVERVIEW AND IMPLICATIONS

Our analysis of the early history of The Boys' Farm both supports and qualifies revisionist arguments as to the impact of the early court and the motives and influence of the associated prominent men. It also provides evidence regarding the relevance and limits of funding considerations as motives for reform-school strategies.

Our analysis of the history of The Boys' Farm from 1950 to 1971 emphasizes the relevance of both its organizational interests and its control over admissions in shaping the disposition of clients. After the mid-1960s, the threat of provincial intervention helped to formalize the informal intergroup relations engendered by the youth-processing organizations' efforts to ward off undesirable clients. The seeds of this threat may be found in the specific links between larger political and economic struggles, the expansion of the welfare state, the influence of treatment-oriented professionals, and the disposition of young clients.

In general, our analysis of the history of The Boys' Farm between 1971 and 1984 supports[12] Lerman's (1982) contention that a new youth-in-trouble system has emerged. According to Lerman, organizations of all three youth-processing networks dealt with an essentially similar and overlapping clientele; that is, with adolescents who can be portrayed as delinquent, neglected, or emotionally disturbed, depending on the needs and interests of the youth-processing organizations. The third section of this book thus emphasizes the impact of these organizations' needs and interests on the disposition of clients, the role of professionals and their treatment-oriented language in facilitating a redefinition of clients and their needs, and the subversion of public policies to various organizational ends.

In 1984,[13] Canada's Juvenile Delinquents Act (1908) was replaced by the Young Offenders Act (1982). On the one hand, that latter act sponsors a renewed concern for justice; on the other, it upholds an expanded concern for diverting youth from contacts with the court. As a result, the Province of Quebec amended its Youth Protection Act in 1984 to return delinquents to the justice system for initial processing.

In the context of these recent policy developments, the concluding chapter emphasizes how the issue of control over admissions is key to understanding how the spirit of public policies gets subverted. Our study tracks the evolution of successful strategies for acquiring control over admissions. It shows how control over admissions is embedded in the changing, local interorganizational environment within which clients are distributed. Finally, it illustrates how studying the history and current operations of local organizational networks can benefit the work of assessing and shaping youth-oriented theories and policies.

METHODS

This book draws together two bodies of research originally conceived and executed as two separate entities. The first is an historical case study by Prue Rains of The Boys' Farm and Training School between 1910 and 1971, conceived in relation to the sociological literature on deviance and social control. The second is a contemporary case study by Eli Teram of Montreal's anglophone youth-protection network after the Quebec Youth Protection Act was implemented in 1979. The latter study was conceived in relation to the social work and sociological literature on human-service organizations, social policy, and interorganizational relations. It was not until we had actually completed our separate pieces of research that we realized the close "fit" between our research sites and independent ways of viewing the politics of client recruitment.

Combining the two studies not only permitted us to document critical developments in the history of one youth-processing organization in a major Canadian city over a remarkably long span of time (1908–84); it also gave us new insights. In particular, our "insider's" perspective on the combined historical and contemporary material helped us to demystify the formal professional rationale for current admissions policies. At the same time, it underlined the impact of this rationale on transforming and legitimating this youth-processing organization and network, at a particular point in history.

The methods used in the historical case study are described briefly in the Appendix; specific sources and additional historical detail are given in the extensive endnotes provided for Parts One and Two. Because the detailed description of the methods used in the qualitative case study, on which Part Three is based, presumes a familiarity with the complexities of the youth-processing networks, we have also discussed these methods at length in the Appendix. The Appendix provides details about the fieldwork sites as well.

PART ONE

Juvenile Justice and The Boys' Farm

Introduction

The advent, in 1908, of Canada's new Juvenile Delinquents Act, authorizing provinces and cities to establish juvenile courts, affected the already existing institutions for delinquent youths in immediate and lasting ways. This introduction reviews the institutions for delinquent boys operating at the time in Montreal, certain key features of the new federal legislation, and the Province of Quebec's first juvenile court in Montreal.

MONTREAL'S REFORM SCHOOLS FOR BOYS

Institutions for delinquent youth in Montreal were established long before juvenile courts. In Canada, federal legislation in 1857[1] permitted the separate punishment of youth; and, by 1859, the first two reformatories for children convicted of crimes had been founded.[2] Until that time, children convicted of criminal offenses served prison sentences with adult offenders at the Provincial Penitentiary in Kingston. These two new juvenile prisons were distinguished from the provincial prison in Kingston only by the age of their inmates (under sixteen years).

Following Confederation in 1867, these institutions were transformed by efforts to "reform the reformatory." The objective was to facilitate the rehabilitation, rather than punishment, of delinquent children through education and useful forms of training in less regimented, more family-like "reform schools" and "industrial schools" (Sutherland 1976, 91–107).[3] As an inevitable result of such efforts, the Ontario Reformatory for Boys at Penetanguishene was reformed, in 1880, and then put out of business by Ontario's newer industrial schools in 1904 (Jones 1978).[4]

In the Province of Quebec, the reformatory at Isle aux Noix was replaced in 1872 by Mont St-Antoine, a Montreal reform school[5] run by the Frères de la Charité[6] under provincial contract. At Mont St-Antoine, francophone Catholic delinquent boys between the ages of fourteen and seventeen were trained in a trade, working eight hours a day in workshops as shoemakers, tailors, and tinsmiths (Tremblay 1984). Even today, Mont St-Antoine is still recognized as the largest reform school (now called reception centres) in both Montreal and the province.

The Boys' Farm and Training School was founded in 1908 to provide a similar alternative to prison for Montreal's anglophone, Protestant, delinquent boys. Housed in a wing of the Sherbrooke Jail, more than a hundred miles from Montreal, "in a room measuring about forty feet by fifteen feet," the boys slept and lived together in the same room, "wearing red jackets and guarded like older criminals" (Citizen, 28 October 1922). When Dr J.J.E. Woods, provincial inspector of reformatories, brought their plight to the attention of the board of directors of Montreal's anglophone Protestant Boys' Home, the directors approached the task with enthusiasm; they did so, however, with an eye for protecting the reputation of the founding institution. "Now, a reformatory school ranks among the penal institutions of the Province, and if the Boys' Home applied for a license as a reformatory school, you can see what would result. The Boys' Home would rank as one of the penal institutions of the Province of Quebec. We cannot afford that. We had to find a means to take up that work in an institution that would be respected by law and which would leave untouched and untarnished the reputation of The Boys' Home."[7] Thus was created the Boys' Farm and Training School. (The two institutions and their respective boards of directors were to separate officially in 1919.)

The founders of The Boys' Farm and Training School were quick to emphasize the contrast between their reform school and prison – especially with regard to the absence of locked doors and fences,[8] and the reforming effects of fresh air, wholesome food, and outdoor work.[9] Established near the village of Shawbridge, forty-three miles north of Montreal, The Boys' Farm sits on 250 acres of farm land, encompassing cultivated land, pasture, mountains, woods, and a river. Indeed, the Farm has always struck observers as a beautiful place, quite unlike a penal institution. In 1908, the new two-storey main building, with turret and balconies, "bore no appearance of a detention Institution" (Dawson 1952, 6).[10] It included accommodation for the staff; a kitchen, dining room, laundry room, and locker room (with individual clothes lockers for each boy); and six dormitories, each housing five boys, on the second floor. Within the first year, a new building for thirty more boys was already under construction.[11] In the early years, boys spent their days doing farm work (five hours) and going to school (three hours), with time set aside for meals, recreation, prayers, and military drill. They got up at 6:00 A.M. and went to bed at 8:30 P.M.

CANADA'S JUVENILE DELINQUENTS ACT (1908)

Two decades of activism in Ontario on behalf of "family-centered care of problem children" culminated in the passage of Canada's Juvenile Delinquents Act in 1908 (Sutherland 1976, 123). During this period, child-saving reformers, such as John J. Kelso,[12] founded children's aid societies geared to placing neglected and dependent children in foster homes rather than institutions (whether industrial schools or orphanages). In addition, the juvenile-court movement promoted separate courts and detention facilities for children, as well as the extension of a family-centred, non-institutional approach to delinquents in the form of supervised probation – a method for supervising children, their parents, and their home environment (Trepanier 1987). The probation officers were given authority to investigate and make recommendations vis-à-vis children before the courts, prior to sentencing. Because these officers could supervise the boys and girls closely, juvenile courts were intended to dispose of most cases through probation. "This movement, in short, wanted to separate children entirely from the whole police and assize court systems and place them in the hands of people whose main interest was in reforming youngsters" (Sutherland 1976, 119).

While influenced directly by American experiments in Chicago,[13] Denver, and Philadelphia,[14] Canada's Juvenile Delinquents Act (1908) had to conform to the constitutional jurisdiction of the federal government, in terms of criminal law, and the provincial governments, in terms of civil matters and the administration of justice. Rather than being defined as a state or condition, as in the United States, delinquency was therefore considered an offence (MacGill 1925, 9); nonetheless, it was broadly defined[15] as the violation, by any child apparently under the age of sixteen, of any "federal, provincial or municipal ordinance for which a fine or imprisonment was the punishment, or any other act for which he or she was liable to be committed to an industrial school or a reformatory" (Sutherland 1976, 121).

Once a province or municipality had established a juvenile court, the court had "the widest possible powers".

First, no matter how serious the case, the juvenile court had jurisdiction over it. Only the court itself could decide to order that an indictable offence be tried before an adult court. Second, once it found a child guilty of delinquency, it had a very wide range of options ... Within the broad framework that it must act as required by 'the child's own good and the best interests of the community', the court could adjourn the hearing, could impose a fine up to ten dollars, could commit the child to the care or custody of a probation officer or other suitable person, could supervise the child through a probation officer in its own home, or could place him in a foster home. Further, it could commit the child to the care of a Children's Aid Society or of a superintendent of neglected and dependent children, or send him to an industrial school, refuge or reformatory. The act, however, specifically forbade that a juvenile delinquent be sentenced to, or incarcerated in any gaol, penitentiary, or police station that also held adults. Even after the court had disposed of the case, the child remained its ward and subject to it until the court itself terminated the relationship or the child became twenty-one years of age." (Sutherland 1976, 122)

Canada's first juvenile courts[16] were established in Winnipeg (1908); in Ottawa, Vancouver, Victoria and Charlottetown (1910); and in Halifax and Toronto (1911).

THE MONTREAL JUVENILE DELINQUENTS COURT

The Province of Quebec established its first juvenile court in Montreal in 1912.[17] Until the late 1930s, the court operated with one part-time judge "who divided his time between the Superior and the Juvenile courts,"[18] and a few overworked and underpaid probation officers. The court's probation service developed along confessional, and thus linguistic, lines. Supported by the Protestant Montreal Juvenile Court Committee,[19] the court named three anglophone women as its first probation officers. By 1935, there were four such officers, "two Catholic, one Protestant, and one Hebrew" (Mendelsohn and Ronald 1969, 50).

There is little systematic information, regarding either the circumstances or the offences, of the youths brought to the new Montreal juvenile court. The clerk of the court's reports for 1914 and 1915 indicate only that boys outnumbered girls by about eight to one, that fourteen was the average age, and that youths were brought to court for a wide range of behaviour, including, but not limited to, crime. Theft and vagrancy were by far the most common offences.[20]

Inasmuch as the new juvenile court supplied all four of Montreal's private reform schools, the court's policies affected all of Montreal's reform schools. Indeed, francophone Catholic delinquents were sent to the two reform schools run by Catholic orders (Mont St-Antoine for boys, Bon Pasteur for girls), and anglophone Protestant delinquents were sent to The Boys' Farm or The Girls' Cottage Industrial School.[21]

CHAPTER TWO

Origins and Management of the 1921–1927 Population Crisis

When the Montreal juvenile court opened in 1912, it was theoretically committed to placing delinquent youths on probation rather than in reform schools. In practice, however, it did both, thereby benefiting the existing reform schools by expanding their client populations, facilities, and budgets. During the first eight years of the court's operation, the number of children in Quebec's reform schools[1] rose steadily – from 367 in 1911 to 678 in 1919 (Table 1). The effect of the court's operation on The Boys' Farm was especially pronounced: from 1911 through 1919, the population more than tripled, going from 42 to 133 boys. As for the court's initial failure to substitute probation for incarceration, that seems to have been a result of the First World War. In effect, reform-school populations rose dramatically during the latter years of the war, as the court attempted to provide a new resource for controlling the wayward children of absent fathers and working mothers.

JUVENILE-COURT POLICY AND THE POPULATION CRISIS

In its early years, the court not only put delinquents on probation; it placed them in reform schools. By the early 1920s, however, probation had clearly become the court's preferred response. Court statistics for 1921 (*Gazette* 1922; *Montreal Star* 1922) show that while the number of children appearing before the court had increased since 1915 (Quebec, *Sessional Papers* 1915), the number of children sent to reform schools had declined – from 159 in 1915, to 92 in 1921.[2] In 1924, Judge J.O. Lacroix of the Montreal juvenile court said: "My first duty is to try to reform the boys and girls through themselves, and I have hundreds under the supervision of my (probation) officers, and many

Table 1
Reform School Population in Quebec (1909–1949)

| Year | Population in all reform schools on Dec. 31 | Population at The Boys' Farm | | |
		Number of committed boys on 1 January	Number of boys committed during year	Number of voluntary boys 1 January	Average total population for year
1909	389	0	46[a]	1	–
1910	376	40	–[b]	–	–
1911	367	42	17	–	–
1912	393	42	43	–	–
1913	446	67	36	–	–
1914	509	86	30	–	–
1915	579	97	53	–	–
1916	475	122	33	–	–
1917	639	133	37	–	–
1918	654	129	44	–	–
1919	678	133	44	–	–
1920	600	132	30	–	147
1921	502	124	15	22	175
1922	404	106	22	71	–
1923	374	82	25	–	–
1924	362	74	17	88	–
1925	426	55	23	80	126
1926	455	59	20	67	121
1927	442	61	31	61	132
1928	455	73	31	59	–
1929	504	78	35	–	–
1930	543	89	34	–	137
1931	586	97	31	–	–
1932	596	106	45	–	–
1933	645	111	39	40	152
1934	693	119	50	–	–
1935	735	126	52	33	165
1936	778	139	35	–	171
1937	761	140	47	–	169
1938	833	138	52	–	171
1939	926	142	57	–	–
1940	909	152	54	14	171
1941	928	160	55	–	169
1942	885	141	94	11	165
1943	952	154	152	7	163
1944	832	162	192	5	169
1945	838	160	182	12	189
1946	670	171	209	13	173
1947	608	139	96	10	143
1948	–	105	62	8	113
1949	–	104	86	5	116

Sources: Figures in the first column are from Quebec, Statistical Yearbooks 1910–1949. Figures in the second column are from Quebec, Sessional Papers 1910–1949. Figures in the third, fourth, and fifth columns are from The Boys' Farm and Training School, Annual Reports.

Notes

a. Boys transferred to The Boys' Farm from other reform schools.

b. A dash indicates unavailable data.

come regularly and report to me. I give them a little talk privately, and in that way help them along the right road. If after a trial of this system I find it is impossible to cure them I will send them away" (*Montreal Star* 1924).

The impact of probation on reform-school populations and budgets was serious. During 1921, the number of boys committed by the Montreal juvenile court to The Boys' Farm dropped by half – from thirty to fifteen; not until 1927 did it reach its former level (Table 1). Thus, from 1921 through 1927, The Boys' Farm faced a population crisis which it, like other reform schools, attributed to the use of probation. Indeed, a member of The Boys' Farm's board of directors observed in 1923, after a visit to two training schools in New York State: "The superintendents of both schools report that the number of boys sent them has declined and this is due to the influence brought to bear on the judges by social workers and others to give the boys more chances on probation" (*Montreal Star* 1923a).

It was in the context of dwindling populations and revenues that the board of directors of The Boys' Farm devised its first strategies for dealing with the impact of the juvenile court on the Farm's client population and budget. The reform school's immediate financial strategies have been detailed elsewhere (Rains 1984). These included the recruitment of Edward W. Beatty, president of the Canadian Pacific Railway, as president of the reform school's board of directors, as well as the successful mobilization of his and other board members' influence[3] on the provincial government to acquire special financial grants. Similar efforts to increase the per diem subsidy, however, did not succeed.[4] Two other strategies that focused more directly on the issue of client recruitment were partially successful: (1) the reform school's use of its status as a private institution to recruit voluntary clients; and (2) the school's mobilization of its board members to use their political influence to lobby the provincial government on behalf of the indefinite sentence.

Recruiting Voluntary Cases

In March 1922, The Boys' Farm took advantage of its status as a private institution to begin not just accepting, but actively recruiting, so-called voluntary cases (boys sent by their parents or relatives rather than by the court). These voluntary cases were considered doubly desirable: not only were they funded privately, usually by their parents, and at rates higher than the provincial per diem rate; but the boys were viewed as more amenable to reform, coming as they did from "more or less respectable homes" (BFTS, board minutes, 26

October 1922). Advertisements for the reform school were placed in magazines; one such advertisement read: "Have you a boy between the ages of 14 and 18, who, in spite of a good home, kind parents, and excellent opportunities, is not doing well? If you have, address a letter to Owen Dawson, Room 629, Transportation Bldg., Montreal. He will tell you where to place this boy for constructive training" (BFTS, scrapbook, 1920–3, *MacLean's Magazine*, undated clipping).

In March and April 1925, the reform school sent 2000 copies of a letter recruiting voluntary cases to ministers of the Presbyterian, Methodist, and Anglican churches in the provinces of Quebec and Ontario. It began: "The Directors of The Boys' Farm and Training School, Shawbridge, Quebec, have decided to add to the number of boarders or voluntary cases, and wish to state that they now have accommodation for an increased number of this class of boys. We have found it to be our experience in the past that parents or guardians of boys needing special training or discipline are often anxious to place their sons in a correctional institution without going through the ordeal of court proceedings" (BFTS, scrapbook, letter dated 27 March 1925).

These private campaigns were effective. During 1922, the number of voluntary cases at The Boys' Farm more than tripled, going from twenty-two to seventy-one, and, initially at least, offsetting the decline in court commitments (Table 1). In 1922, revenue from these voluntary cases stood at $21,000, having risen from $5,000 in 1920. Between 1922 and 1927 (data are scarce for 1928 and 1929), voluntary cases comprised from 40 to 60 per cent of the client population – which nevertheless continued to decline – and brought in from $20,000 to $30,000 a year.

As part of a strategy for bypassing the juvenile court, the Farm's recruitment of voluntary cases took advantage of the school's status as a private institution. The school, in fact, encouraged institutionalization as a parental response to anxieties over the control of adolescent boys. Perhaps parents were grasping, as well, for solutions to the more general hardships of their lives, solutions formal commitments could at times provide. As one reporter wrote:

Willie's incarceration at Shawbridge, according to his mother, came as the result of her own application to the Seigneur Street police station, Montreal, two years ago when the child disappeared from home and she sought help from the police to bring him back. "He ran away because his father was a brute at home," she states. "My husband was drinking a lot. He was not working, and I was going out by day as a charwoman trying to earn money to keep us in food and lodging. Willie was terrified of his father and he used to run away. So I went to the police station and asked them to find him for me. Detective Brooks found him and he was taken to the Juvenile Court. I was glad to think of him going out to Shawbridge, because I thought it would be a good place for him to be." After a month at a reformatory in the city, Willie Hayes was sentenced to three years at Shawbridge on the charge of "desertion from home." The date of his sentence was January 23rd, 1922.[5]

The recruitment of voluntary clients remained a staple institutional strategy for increasing client populations when necessary, until offset by the rising costs of institutional care.[6]

Implementing the Indefinite Sentence

The federal Juvenile Delinquents Act (1908) did not mention the indefinite sentence directly; nor did the detailed commentaries on the federal legislation by its authors and promoters (MacGill 1925; W.L. Scott 1930). Moreover, the Quebec legislation (1910), because it simply proclaimed the federal act as relevant to Quebec and authorized the creation of a juvenile court in Montreal, had no reason to mention the indefinite sentence directly. Yet the federal Juvenile Delinquents Act also failed to mention definite sentences. Indeed, juvenile justice reformers, and the text of the legislation itself, so clearly favoured methods other than incarceration for dealing with delinquents, that the commitment of delinquents to reform schools was itself scarcely mentioned. Nevertheless, the indefinite sentence was a core tenet in the movement to reform, rather than punish, delinquents. It was implicit in the discretionary powers and the wardship-hold over youth given the juvenile court by the act, as well as in the law's provision, that the court should not authorize the release of delinquents without a recommendation from the reform school. The intent of this provision was to permit reform schools to release delinquents when successfully reformed, rather than at some arbitrary date; fully implemented, this provision would have transferred control over the length of delinquents' sentences from the juvenile court to the reform school.

Judges at the Montreal juvenile court were reluctant to sentence delinquents to indefinite terms. In 1922, the superintendent of The Boys' Farm observed at a board meeting that indefinite sentences were not being used by judges at Montreal's juvenile court. Moreover, in 1924, the secretary-treasurer of the reform school reported that a newly appointed judge of the Montreal court was "not a believer in the Indefinite Sentence as provided by the Juvenile Delinquents Act" (BFTS, board minutes, 31 January 1924). Judges at the Montreal court, however, were not only trained as lawyers but worked in courts other than the juvenile court; because they continued to adhere to an older model of justice, they were reluctant to turn their control regarding length of sentence over to the reform schools.

In 1922, during its first serious population crisis, The Boys' Farm began to lobby for the indefinite sentence, bringing the considerable influence of its elite board members to bear on the provincial government. In March 1922, E.W. Beatty, then-president of The Boys' Farm (and the Canadian Pacific Railway), reported to the board that "he had gone into the question of the indefinite sentence with (Quebec premier) Taschereau, the Provincial Secretary, and Sir Lomer Gouin (former Quebec premier), all of whom were in favor of the plan"[7] (BFTS, board minutes, 8 March 1922). The reform school favoured indefinite sentences for two reasons: as a strategy for increasing its control over troublesome clients and as a strategy for increasing its client population.

Increased internal control.   In the early 1900s, all reform schools in Quebec objected to government pardons, arguing that early release (parole) should depend on good conduct alone. The Boys' Farm's preference for the indefinite sentence was thus partly an extension of that earlier effort to gain control over the decision to release or parole. (Because release did not depend on behaviour, the school argued that definite sentences limited the effectiveness of parole as a device for maintaining internal control.)

In the early 1920s, The Boys' Farm made persistent, and largely unsuccessful, attempts to persuade the provincial secretary to extend the sentences of boys "unfit for discharge." In June 1922, for example, "the Superintendent submitted a list of 14 boys whose time expires before the close of this year and who were entirely unfit for discharge. He recommended that the provincial Secretary be requested to extend their terms. The President (Beatty) reported that he had an appointment with the Hon. Mr. David (the provincial secretary) for the following morning, when he would request him to grant a temporary extension of the terms of the boys referred to until their cases could be more carefully studied" (BFTS, board minutes, 21 June 1922). But, four months later, Beatty reported that the request for the extension of the terms of the fourteen boys at the Farm had been refused by the provincial secretary. "The question had (subsequently) been a matter of serious discussion between himself (Beatty) and (Taschereau) and the Hon. Walter Mitchell (provincial treasurer). The (premier) requested that in future all such matters be taken up direct with him" (BFTS, board minutes, 26 October 1922).

Because The Boys' Farm only occasionally succeeded in having the sentences of individual boys extended, it turned to the indefinite sentence as a way of gaining control over the release, and therefore the conduct, of its more troublesome clients.

Increased client population.   The client population at The Boys' Farm could be increased by either more court commitments or longer sentences. The reform school's efforts to lengthen the sentences of boys it viewed as unfit for discharge therefore addressed the twin issues of client population and internal control. But the length of sentences was of concern for still another reason. The Montreal juvenile court, with its increased implementation of the principles of the juvenile-justice movement, not only was augmenting its use of probation as a substitute for reform-school commitment, but was also reducing sentences for those it did commit – from the previous three-to-five-year period down to two years or less.[8] In effect, shorter sentences amplified the impact of probation on The Boys' Farm's client population. This meant that the reform school, although it could not reasonably hope to increase its client population by opposing the use of probation, could at least hope to increase its population by invoking the Juvenile Delinquents Act of 1908, thereby gaining control over the lengths of its clients' sentences.

In 1924, faced with the judges' continued resistance to awarding indefinite sentences, The Boys' Farm planned a legal challenge to the definite sentence. Walter Mitchell, provincial treasurer under both Gouin and Taschereau and, by this time, a member of the reform school's board of directors, offered not only to seek the legal opinion of his former law partner, N.K. Laflamme, but also to take the matter up with Quebec's attorney general. In February 1924, Laflamme reported to the board that he "believed that the Judge of the Juvenile Court had the option of giving an indefinite sentence under the Juvenile Delinquents Act, or a definite sentence of not less than two or more than five years under the old Prisons and Reformatories Act." Mr. Laflamme stated further that, in his opinion, "any definite term of less than two years was illegal" (BFTS, board minutes, 28 February 1924). The board agreed to take the matter up with the attorney general after the legislative session ended in Quebec and, once a "parole board" had been created within the reform school, "to deal with the discharge of committed cases" (BFTS, board minutes, 27 March 1924).[9]

Four months later, the board planned to convey the legal opinion it had solicited to the Montreal court: "The question of short-term sentences was discussed and it was agreed to admit boys from the

Juvenile Court for short terms in the meantime. The Secretary was asked to convey the opinion of Mr. N.K. Laflamme in this connection to the Juvenile Court authorities and if no satisfactory conclusion was reached to take the matter up with the Hon. Walter Mitchell" (BFTS, board minutes, 26 June 1924).

The Boys' Farm, although unsuccessful in convincing the court to use the indefinite sentence,[10] did persuade the court to extend definite sentences. Records for boys discharged between May 1939 and May 1941 (they therefore had been sentenced in the mid-1930s) show that these boys were sentenced for definite, rather than indefinite, terms. None of the 143 sentences, however, were for less than 2 years and most were for 3, 4, and 5 years (the mean sentence was 3.67 years). The reform school appears, therefore, to have succeeded temporarily in holding off the threat of short sentences for its client population. Moreover, as attested to by the following note in The Boys' Farm board minutes, it succeeded in acquiring recognition of its right to be consulted by the court regarding the actual release date of sentenced clients: "Colonel Magee (a board member) reported that he had had a very satisfactory interview with Judge Lacroix (of the Juvenile Court) in reference to the releasing of the Wilson boys (two brothers). The Judge has promised that he would not release any more boys without first asking for a report from the Farm management" (BFTS, board minutes, 30 October 1924).

By 1930, the first population crisis was over at The Boys' Farm as well as the province's other reform schools (the largest of these being the two French-Catholic reform schools in Montreal, also supplied by the Montreal juvenile court). Although longer sentences had contributed to the growth in population, increased court commitments were the major contributing factor. Indeed, by 1927, the number of court commitments to The Boys' Farm had risen to pre-1920 levels, and the climb continued through 1946. It seems that court commitments accelerated during the depression years after 1929, suggesting that both the court and the reform school were being called upon to deal with the social and family problems created by unemployment and financial stress. Subsequently, between 1930 and 1946, the population of the province's reform schools reached record levels; at The Boys' Farm, for example, there were more than 200 inhabitants.

IMPLICATIONS FOR THE REVISIONIST DEBATE

Recent debates in the United States and Canada concerning the turn-of-the-century invention known as the "juvenile court" have pitted revisionists against counter-revisionists. Contentions abound as to the nature of the court, its sponsors, and its impact on youths (Igna-tieff 1981, Mennel 1983). For example, was the new juvenile court a class-sponsored device to extend state control over the children of immigrant working-class families, or something more benign? The early history of relations between the Montreal juvenile court and The Boys' Farm sheds light on three issues involved in these debates: (1) the impact of the invention of juvenile courts on the incarceration of youth; (2) the involvement of members of the business and indus-trial elite in juvenile-justice policy; and (3) the survival of reform schools in the face of juvenile-court policies.

The Impact of the New Juvenile Court

Although the newly created (1912) juvenile court in Montreal put many children on probation, it also clearly increased the number of children in reform schools. This fact supports revisionist claims (Platt 1969)[11] concerning the impact of the new court introduced in Chicago in 1899; however, it also contradicts the counter-revisionist claims made for Canada (Hagan and Leon 1977)[12] as to the impact of the new court instituted in Toronto in 1912.

The new juvenile court in Montreal initially facilitated the incar-ceration of youths during the First World War, when both the court and reform schools could be called upon to absorb the unsupervised, problem children of absent fathers and working mothers. In this respect, it is significant that Hagan and Leon's (1977) data for the early Toronto juvenile court – founded in the same year as the Mon-treal court – do not include the years of the First World War, when the court was most likely to have incarcerated children.[13] At the same time, their evidence that the Toronto court employed probation rather than incarceration during the 1920s is consistent with the trend of the Montreal data. (Their data also indicate, as do ours, a significant increase in reform-school commitments during the Second World War.[14]) Their contention – that Canadian juvenile courts differed from their American counterparts in emphasizing probation and informal, rather than criminalizing, methods of social control – may, in fact, not only overstate national differences between the two countries' juvenile courts but understate the relevance of other explanations for juvenile-court practices.[15]

Elite Involvement in Juvenile-Justice Policy

The early history of The Boys' Farm qualifies revisionist arguments about the motives and influence of prominent men in juvenile-justice policy. As Montreal's only English reform school for boys, The Boys'

Farm attracted considerable charity from prominent English Montreal businessmen who served on its board of directors. In that capacity, they worked hard to influence juvenile-justice policy, particularly regarding the issue of the indefinite sentence. Their efforts, however, reflected more a commitment to making a pet charity work, rather than an ulterior interest in turning delinquent boys into docile and disciplined industrial workers – as some have argued. Indeed, board members volunteered their services as a matter of conscience, out of a general – if increasingly inaccurate – view of The Boys' Farm as an alternative to prison for young, wayward, and still reformable, boys. What they had to offer as board members were their social contacts and "know-how" in making enterprises work.[16] In that sense, they employed their values and skills to ensure the financial viability and continued existence of The Boys' Farm, rather than to affect the boys themselves.

The Boys' Farm's first population crisis occurred at a time when the power of Montreal's English elite and its influence vis-à-vis the provincial government were considerable. Indeed, Montreal's "Anglo-Scottish commercial and financial elite built and still controls some of Canada's major economic institutions" (Behiels 1985, 13), and "a close working relationship between government and business was a long-established tradition in Quebec politics. In fact, to facilitate this relationship it had been customary for the Provincial Treasurer to be a Montreal anglophone who was a member of the Montreal financial community" (McRoberts 1988, 107–8).[17] Connections like these helped to enlist provincial government support for The Boys' Farm during its early years. During the 1940s and 1950s, however, this privileged support for a relatively costly English institution was to fade. The active involvement of prominent men in charitable work would also fade during the late 1960s, when psychiatric and social work professionals alike acquired greater authority over social services. In the 1920s, however, the board of directors of The Boys' Farm was well placed to lobby for changes in juvenile-justice policy.

The board's lack of success is perhaps as notable, therefore, as their success. In fact, the board did manage to obtain more money from the province, to forestall the court's movement toward shorter sentences, and to persuade the court to recognize the reform school's right to be consulted regarding the release of boys. It failed, however, to have the indefinite sentence implemented and to acquire control over the release date of the boys, even though both policies were implicit in federal legislation. These failures demonstrate how The Boys' Farm, in spite of unusual organizational resources, was unable to affect the operation of the court. Even the court's willingness to reinstate longer sentences could be justified in the court's own terms for, by the 1930s, long sentences seemed an appropriate response to the failure of older boys on probation.

Survival of Reform Schools

The Boys' Farm both profited and suffered from its dependence on the juvenile court for clients. Its first population crisis shows that such court policies as probation and shortened sentences did, in fact, affect reform schools more seriously than revisionist views have implied. It is also clear, however, that The Boys' Farm actively resisted the impact of juvenile-court policy on the size of its client population, thereby contributing to its own net-widening. The recruitment of voluntary cases, for instance, encouraged beleaguered parents to place problem youngsters in reform school, thus drawing youths not in trouble with the law into the institution. Although activism on behalf of the indefinite sentence did not succeed in lengthening the sentences of committed boys, activism against shortened sentences did, thus partially counteracting the decarcerating policies of the court. Evidently the reasons for net-widening and *how* it occurs are likely to be found in just such local histories of organizational resistance.

CHAPTER THREE

Last-Resort Disposition of Older Delinquents, 1942–1966

Reforms designed to replace the incarceration of delinquents with milder alternatives affect not only the size but also the composition of reform-school populations. In other words, reform-school clients become the older "recidivists," who have failed in milder alternatives and now replace the more desirable clients the reform school once served. The juvenile court's preference for placing delinquents on probation, often several times, meant that delinquents arrived at reform schools at older ages than was once the case. In the Province of Quebec, the juvenile court's jurisdiction was limited to youth under sixteen until 1942, and to youth under eighteen thereafter. But because the court had the right to supervise youth who had appeared before it up to the age of twenty-one, the court often committed delinquents older than sixteen or eighteen to reform schools. By the mid-1930s, the Montreal juvenile court was committing boys over the age of sixteen to The Boys' Farm, and their numbers increased in 1942, when the Province of Quebec extended the age of juveniles to eighteen.

PUBLIC POLICY AND THE OPPOSITION OF REFORM SCHOOLS

Reform schools[1] opposed the admission of older boys and the age-extension legislation, hoping that separate institutions for sixteen- to eighteen-year-olds would be created. In fact, the aging of reform school populations had already occurred in provinces such as Ontario, where well-developed probation services were in place before the juvenile court was even created (Hagan and Leon 1977). It was in 1921 – when the federal minister of justice, at the urging of the Canadian Council of Child Welfare and other juvenile-justice reformers, introduced an amendment to the federal Juvenile Delinquents Act that would raise the age of juveniles from sixteen to eighteen – that Ontario's reform schools complained. They saw the age extension as a policy that would simply exaggerate the process already at work; that is, the commitment to their institutions of an increasingly older group of repeat offenders. Their position was that age-extension legislation should wait until new and more prisonlike reform schools could be created specifically for this older group. (The English Borstal institutions for young offenders between the ages of sixteen and twenty-one were favoured as a model.[2]) Their resistance to the amendment successfully blocked the proposed *mandatory* extension of age. Instead, the amendment granted *discretionary* authority to provinces to extend the age from sixteen to eighteen (Canada 1921, House of Commons, Debates, 1069 and 3319; Scott 1930, 8).

The age-extension issue continued to pit the interests of reform schools against the convictions of juvenile-justice reformers, who had hoped to extend the benefits of juvenile justice to older "children." In 1938, The Royal Commission to Investigate the Penal System of Canada completed two years of hearings and investigations into the Canadian penitentiary system, including the system for dealing with juvenile offenders. The Archambault report (named after the chair of the commission) said:

Many conflicting representations were made to the Commission as to whether the age limit of those to come under the jurisdiction of the juvenile courts should be raised throughout Canada to include young persons below the age of eighteen years. Your Commissioners are definitely of the opinion that the jurisdiction of the juvenile courts should be limited to children below the age of sixteen years ... The problem of detention homes and training schools would be clearly aggravated, and, in our opinion, has been aggravated (in British Columbia and Manitoba) where the age limit has been increased. (Canada 1938, 188)

THE BOYS' FARM AND OLDER BOYS

Administrators at The Boys' Farm also viewed older boys as undesirable clients. Older boys were seen as being more difficult to control: they ran away, required extended school programs, or perhaps were old enough to be free of compulsory school requirements altogether.[3] The Boys' Farm also blamed its periodic population and financial crises on these older clients. Its administrators knew that the judges, having sent older boys to the reform school, were then often reluctant to expose younger "normal bad boys" to this bad influence. The client population was accordingly both altered and reduced. To make matters worse, the increased incidence of commitment of older boys to The Boys' Farm did not necessarily offset the reduced commitment of younger boys; also older boys ran away, thus costing the reform school the per diem payments from the province. The reform school therefore hoped to ward off the commitment of older boys.

Controlling the Disposition of Older Delinquents

The Boys' Farm employed three strategies in its efforts to control the commitment of older delinquents. First, its board of directors refused to build a locked unit for chronic runaways, despite pressure to do so from the Farm's own superintendents and the court itself. Second, it joined with Montreal's other reform schools and the Montreal juvenile court in pressing the province to build a new institution for older delinquents. Third, it tried to resist the court's tricky use of the reform school as a "gateway to the penitentiary" for older runaways.

The locked detention-unit conflict.   Since its opening in 1908, the open-door policy of The Boys' Farm, as well as its lack of fences, had been central to the Farm's "non-prison" image. Indeed, its country location, so far from Montreal,[4] was expected to discourage runaways and facilitate recapture. The first two boys who ran away, in 1909, were thus dealt with severely as an example.[5] The Boys' Farm controlled runaways in three ways: through revocation of their early release time, through corporal punishment, and through short-term confinement in the nearby St-Jerome Jail or at Bordeaux Jail in Montreal. In 1935, when overcrowding and increased numbers of older boys led to unusually large numbers of runaways, Superintendent Ralph Willcock (1928–42)[6] proposed that a "detention room" be created as an alternative way of dealing with "repeated absconders."

The runaway problem escalated during the Second World War (1943–46) when increased commitments led to overcrowded conditions.[7] Noting that there were 187 runaways in 1943, and 207 during the first ten months of 1944, a researcher reported: "(to) 'runaway' is one of the most serious offences at the Farm. It is also one of its most serious problems and still awaits a solution. Homesickness is given more often than any other reason for running away.[8] Boys who have received a severe strapping from one of the cottage parents will seek their revenge by running away. When one goes he is usually accompanied by one or two of his companions. They believe in 'sticking together'" (Nearing 1945, 39). In fact, during the first eight months of 1946, when more than half the boys in residence at The Boys' Farm were sixteen years or older, 121 boys ran away a total of 230 times, at an estimated loss of $2,000 in per diem payments.

The new superintendent,[9] George Young (1945–48),[10] argued for "two detention rooms" on the grounds that corporal punishment was ineffective:

The use of corporal punishment is in vogue in cases of all runaways ... this mode of punishment is not being really effective ... We have one boy who has run away, or attempted to run away, 8 times since January 25th. This boy has been subjected to corporal punishment repeatedly, and on the last occasion it was administered by the Superintendent to an extent that was considered almost excessive. Within 48 hours of this punishment being administered this boy ran away again – which simply proves the ineffectiveness of this type of punishment. (BFTS, internal correspondence, Young, Memorandum Re Detention Facilities at The Boys' Farm, 17 March 1947)

In response, The Boys' Farm's board of directors argued that the existence of locked units would legitimate the court's use of the reform school as a dumping ground for older delinquents. The president of the committee set up to discuss the possibility refused Superintendent Young's request: "I conclude that you are prepared to accept a certain type of the older group of boys provided there are some facilities established for solitary confinement at the Farm. Am I also right in concluding that we would have no legitimate excuse or justification for refusing to accept the older age group should they be committed to the Farm? If I am correct, it looks as if we must resort to some other means of solving your difficulty" (BFTS, board minutes, 30 April 1947).[11]

In 1950, the new provincial child welfare legislation permitted The Boys' Farm to receive court-committed "protection" cases as well as delinquents. The development of the Province of Quebec's child-welfare system, and its impact on The Boys' Farm, are examined in the next section of this book. In the context of the efforts of The Boys' Farm to ward off the commitment of older delinquents, the new legislation was significant: for a time, at least, it generated hopes that the older delinquents would be replaced by more desirable youth protection cases. There were new hopes, as well, that the province would build a separate institution for older delinquents.

The question of a "closed" institution.   Montreal's reform schools[12] and juvenile court were united in pressing for a new institution to deal with older delinquent runaways. While early advocates envisioned a separate institution for all sixteen- to eighteen-year-old delinquents, later advocates envisioned a "closed" institution that existing reform schools could use as a temporary backup for their difficult cases, particularly runaways. In 1956, the Quebec Conference on Youth Protection Schools[13] recommended construction of a closed institution to house 150 boys and 50 girls in units of fifteen, with two units reserved for English-speaking boys. Although construction of the resulting maximum-security juvenile prison began in 1958, Centre Berthelet did not go into full operation for another ten years.[14]

With hopes stalled for a separate institution for older delinquents, the issue of a locked unit at The Boys' Farm was revived, both at the reform school and within the court. A vicious circle had been set in motion: once apprehended, the runaways would reappear before the Montreal juvenile court; the judges would then return them to the reform school where – in the absence of a locked unit – they continued to run away and reappear before the court. The judges accordingly became increasingly insistent that a locked unit be instituted at The Boys' Farm. In 1962, the reform school's court representative reported to the executive director, "Whilst in court today, Judge Long asked me what it would cost in dollars and cents to convert The Boys' Farm into a security school. I was more than slightly amazed at such a question and informed the Judge that this was a matter that our Board would have certain views about" (BFTS, internal correspondence, Aldersley, 12 January 1962).

A year later, Superintendent A.L. Evans (1948–67)[15] also advocated a "separate unit with security features," on the grounds that runaways were the "main cause of the drop in population" during 1961 and 1962:[16] "The seriousness of the AWOL situation in 1961 was referred to in the Annual Report and, as is indicated this year with a greater figure of 44 for the first 10 months, accounts for our present drop in the number of boys in residence. There is no need for me to point out the great loss in revenue caused by the absence of this number … if we are unable to control the AWOL trend of 1961 and this year, the average annual population will continue downwards" (BFTS, internal correspondence, Evans, 23 January 1963). As Evans pointed out, most of the runaways were older delinquent boys, and half had run away three or more times. The board of directors was still reluctant, however, to embark on this "departure from our lifetime policy" and the "type of institution we cherish."[17]

The penitentiary debate.   The long-term stalemate between judges at the Montreal juvenile court and the board of directors of The Boys' Farm over the creation of a locked unit led the court to devise its own strategy. The goal was to force the reform school to assume responsibility for the disposition of older runaways.

Without a separate institution for older delinquents or locked units at The Boys' Farm, the judges had few options for dealing with boys who repeatedly ran away. Under the provisions of the Juvenile Delinquents Act, they could refer boys older than fourteen to the adult court and thus to the penitentiary. But the judges preferred not to exercise this option; the adult court often simply released such boys on probation as "first offenders" (first offenders in the adult system), thus encouraging runaways.[18]

Juvenile-court judges, themselves, did not have authority to send boys to the penitentiary. Under Canada's Prisons and Reformatories Act, however, an "industrial school" like The Boys' Farm could apply to the juvenile court for removal of an uncontrollable inmate "to a place of stricter confinement" for the remainder of his term.[19] The Boys' Farm had used this procedure, as early as 1946,[20] for the detention of older runaways in the St-Jerome and Bordeaux Jails.[21] Thus the judges had a third option: they could send boys to the penitentiary without turning them over to the adult courts. That step required an application from the reform school, however, requesting the boy's removal "to a place of stricter confinement." In the early 1960s, the Montreal juvenile court seized the initiative in using this procedure: judges began to announce to boys that failure to stay at The Boys' Farm would mean that the reform school would make an application for their removal to the penitentiary. When boys did run away and reappeared before the court, the judges privately requested the reform school to request a removal and then held a court hearing at which they "agreed" to send boys to the penitentiary.

In 1963, Judges Nicholson and Long devised a new "legal gimmick" to strengthen the threat of this procedure. Instead of returning runaways to the reform school under the original indefinite sentence, the judges began to recommit the boys on definite sentences.[22] When recommitted boys ran away again, the judges could then use the reform school's ensuing application to send them to the penitentiary for the remainder of the definite terms. In effect, when Judge Long began to recommit boys in this way for definite terms ranging from thirty months to three years, he was sending runaways to the adult penitentiary for much longer terms than either those of the indefinite commitments[23] to The Boys' Farm (there indefinite sentences were interpreted as twelve to fifteen months), or those they would have served in the adult penitentiary (if the boys had been sent to and sentenced by the adult court).

Although The Boys' Farm objected to the court's use of reform schools as a "gateway to the penitentiary," it did not want to alienate the court it depended on for clients. In 1965, the reform school's court representative reported:

On Monday, The Boys' Farm received six boys, some of whom are under 30 months definite commitment, and have already been told that if they run away or misbehave "The Boys' Farm would make an application to have them transferred to the penitentiary." The right to make this request is the pre-rogative of the school, not the court. The act was designed to protect the school, not provide a means to send a boy to penitentiary – the easy way. The boy goes to penitentiary for something he failed to do: stay at The Boys' Farm ...

Frankly, when I am asked in open court whether the application is well founded and I answer "yes" under oath, I perjure myself. Further I am fully aware that the application was made at the request of the court, not The Boys' Farm, and in an effort not to offend the court, I am fully responsible for any sentence that may be imposed – 42 months with no parole in the last case.

I have a conscience, Mr. Weir,[24] and I know that in the not too distant future one of these new boys will run away, and I know that the judge will ask for application under 217. And if there are no behavior reports of violence to other boys or staff, or behavior "endangering the general discipline of the school" (and this does not mean one AWOL), I am afraid that I will be forced to refuse to give evidence in open court in any one of these cases. As I understand my job, it is to keep boys out of prison, not put them in – especially for the sake of good relations and the convenience of the Court. (BFTS, internal correspondence, Aldersley, 4 February 1965)

In a meeting with provincial officials on 16 February 1965, the reform school argued that the definite-commitment "gimmick" was illegal. A month later, the Montreal juvenile-court judges abandoned definite commitments, but continued to use the removal-application procedure in conjunction with indefinite commitments.

The reform school then adopted a counter-strategy of its own: it began to refuse to apply for removals, hoping to force the judges either to hold older runaways in the court's detention centre, or to refer them to the adult court. In response to one such refusal, Judge

Nicholson wrote a six-page plea in favour of the removal-application procedure, ending with the implied threat that refusal to use the procedure might open the reform school to "possible liability for the boy's actions in the event of the school being held at fault for failure to take the steps open to it to have him placed in closer custody" (BFTS, internal correspondence, Nicholson, 25 June 1966). A month later, the reform school's court representative reported Judge Nicholson's reaction to The Boys' Farm's refusal to make a removal-application for another boy: "He has a great deal of respect and thanks Mr. Evans[25] who, for years, has always been so cooperative, and *it must be with a* GREAT DEAL OF DISAPPOINTMENT THAT HE *(Evans) will eventually have to realize that the law is the law and provide the means for The Boys' Farm to select their boys* ... He asked that further consideration be given to an application for transfer and adjourned the case to July 14th" (BFTS, internal correspondence, Aldersley, 7 July 1966; emphasis in original).

From 1946 through 1966, The Boys' Farm successfully used its authority as a private institution to refuse locked units for the control of older runaways; it failed, however, to deter judges from using the reform school as a placement for older delinquents. In 1966, the refusal of The Boys' Farm to use the removal-application procedure seriously alienated the judges they depended upon for commitments. In 1966 and 1967, the number of delinquent boys committed to the Farm dropped significantly: from seventy-four in 1965, to forty-six in 1966 and forty-five in 1967 (Table 2).[26] The low population, in combination with the increasing numbers of boys being held in the Montreal juvenile-court's detention centre, led to ever more critical inquiries from the province. Indeed, in 1966, The Boys' Farm, as an institution, was dying. This came about because of its strategies not only of trying to control the disposition of older delinquents, but also of trying to manage and control the disposition of emotionally disturbed protection cases (to be discussed in chapter 4).

PRODUCING OLDER TROUBLE-MAKERS

The long struggle between The Boys' Farm and the Montreal juvenile court over the disposition of older delinquents calls attention to four issues: (1) the effects of juvenile-court policy on the composition of reform-school populations and the control of clients; (2) the sources and costs of organizational resistance to court control over the disposition of clients; (3) the countervailing practices that, despite the

Table 2
Population at The Boys' Farm (1950-1970)

Year	Number of committed boys on 1 January	Number of boys committed during year (YPSA/JDA)*		Re-admissions	Average total population for year
1950	103	88		17	134
1951	137	74		5	136
1952	130	90		7	141
1953	136	99		7	151
1954	140	50		9	133
1955	114	54		9	125
1956	119	86		14	122
1957	117	98	(64/44)	22	124
1958	111	124	(51/72)	21	135
1959	131	119	(52/67)	26	152
1960	148	89	(37/52)	12	150
1961	140	104	(35/69)	15	135
1962	127	110	(39/71)	21	125
1963	107	124	(58/66)	10	133
1964	125	115	(55/60)	29	133
1965	131	115	(41/74)	26	129
1966	114	87	(41/46)	14	96
1967	96	82	(37/45)	22	104
1968	110	–		–	86
1969	70	–		–	–
1970	62	–		–	68

Source: The Boys' Farm, Annual reports, 1950-70 (except for 1963 and 1966). Data for 1963 are reconstituted from internal statistical reports and records, for 1966 from the Shamsie report. Average total population figures have been rounded off to the nearest whole number and include a relatively small but steady number of readmissions, recommitments, or voluntary cases not counted as "new admissions."

Note * Where reported, the number of new admissions committed as protection cases under the provincial Youth Protection Schools Act (YPSA) are distinguished from new admissions committed as delinquents under the federal Juvenile Delinquents Act (JDA).

movement to mitigate the treatment of juvenile offenders, selected some juvenile offenders for treatment as criminal adults; and (4) the impact of these struggles on clients.

Effects of Juvenile Court Policy on Reform-School Populations

The aging of reform-school populations[27] may reflect certain social and demographic changes regarding the availability of eligible clients: increased numbers of boys in the upper end of the juvenile age-range;[28] increases in the number or seriousness of their delinquent offenses;[29] or increases in the amount of official attention being paid to the activities of older boys. But the aging of reform-school populations also reflects public policy (the extension of the juvenile age from sixteen to eighteen) and juvenile-court policy (the preferred use of probation). Indeed, reforms designed to replace incarceration with milder alternatives do affect institutional populations. By reserving institutions for system "failures," who come equipped with the experience and reputation that accompanies such failure, a change occurs in the composition of institutional populations. That change is used, in turn, to justify intensified control over clients and the countervailing practices discussed below.

Sources and Costs of Organizational Resistance

For many years, The Boys' Farm's board of directors tried to resist the court's transformation of its client population by refusing to create a locked detention unit. The board was well aware that virtually all reform schools in the United States and Canada had locked facilities; indeed, the superintendents at The Boys' Farm repeatedly advocated creating a locked unit on just those grounds. The board's resistance was anomalous, intentionally strategic, and indicative of the power that boards of directors continued to have over private institutions such as The Boys' Farm. Fundamentally, the reform school's private board of directors was unwilling to solve its financial, population, and internal control problems by sacrificing its traditional orientation ("our lifetime policy") toward the reform of "normal bad boys." Nevertheless, they agreed that the thought that "our population no longer represents a normal cross-section of needy boys ... tends to disturb, if not perhaps change, the very nature of our school which we are so jealous to preserve."[30] Board members were removed, however, from the day-to-day operation of the reform school. It was the superintendents who had to deal more immediately with the problems of control that runaways in particular presented. Equipped only with corporal punishment as a tool for dealing with these problems, the superintendents favoured locked units as an alternative.[31] But whereas board members could control superintendents, they could not control the court, and, in the end, their refusal of the types of clients they *could* get almost put The Boys' Farm out of business. The history of their struggle to ward off undesirable clients clearly illustrates the costs of resisting the court's authority.

Treating Older Boys as Criminals

Over the years, many policies have been designed to treat juvenile delinquents separately and less harshly than adult offenders. Reform schools have been created to remove young offenders from adult penitentiaries. Juvenile courts and juvenile-court detention centres have been established to remove youths from adult courts and jails. Reform schools have been organized around family-like cottages to remove youths from the prisonlike atmosphere of juvenile reformatories. In addition, sixteen- to eighteen-year-olds have been redefined as juveniles, thereby entitling more adolescents to these forms of special treatment.

Of course, many studies have demonstrated how these measures unintentionally produced harsher treatment than that awarded to adolescents whose offences were mitigated by their youth in the adult justice and corrections system. For example, more adolescents were incarcerated, and for longer periods of time and milder offences. Few studies, however, have examined the countervailing practices whereby certain adolescents were intentionally selected as recipients of harsher treatment, as adults. In this chapter, we have expressly documented three such countervailing practices: (1) the option of juvenile-court judges to refer adolescents over the age of fourteen to the adult court;[32] (2) the option of juvenile-court judges to send older adolescents to adult penitentiaries when petitioned to do so by reform schools; and, (3) the expansion of prisonlike facilities for adolescents at the "deep end" of the juvenile delinquency network (these include "closed" institutions for older offenders, the development of locked units within "open" institutions, and the expansion of locked detention facilities).

These relatively unnoticed and countervailing practices are usually justified as measures for protecting the community from the serious offences of older adolescents. Our evidence that these practices were promoted as methods for "holding" runaways shows how social-control organizations, in solving their own problems, may actually penalize young "system nuisances" who simply resist social control[33] rather than commit serious crimes. In other words, the redefinition of sixteen- to eighteen-year-olds as juveniles, as well as the movement to decarcerate delinquent adolescents, has masked several practices for sending older adolescents to prison.

Impact on Clients

The long struggle between The Boys' Farm and the Montreal juvenile court over the disposition of older delinquents had a direct impact on clients: it encouraged the use of corporal punishment, the development of spectacularly high runaway rates,[34] the emergence of juvenile prisons (Centre Berthelet), and the dispatch of older persistent runaways to penitentiaries.

We also speculate that the creation of new juvenile prisons has meant new locations for the organizational processes just described. That is, efforts by these new institutions to maintain the size of client populations, if successful, simply draw more clients deeper into the juvenile delinquency network. Also, efforts to control the composition of client populations, if successful, recruit desirable clients. In the end, however, The Boys' Farm failed to recruit the "normal bad boys" it had once served. Moreover, its refusal to deal with a new clientele contributed to the definition and treatment of these less desired clients as "young criminals".

PART TWO

Youth Protection
and The Boys' Farm

Introduction

Having examined policies affecting the disposition of delinquent youth and their impact on The Boys' Farm from 1912 to 1966 in the first section of this book, we now focus on the policies affecting the disposition of child-welfare cases and their impact on The Boys' Farm from 1950 to the late 1960s. The disposition of delinquents could be understood as an outcome of juvenile-court decisions and attempts by The Boys' Farm to influence these decisions. The disposition of child-welfare cases, in contrast, must be understood in a broader context – one involving other child-welfare agencies as well as the court. Our re-examination of the period after 1950 is done in light of the new dynamics created by the redefinition of reform schools as youth-protection schools.

In 1950, the Province of Quebec's new Youth Protection Schools Act altered the placement of neglected youth by allowing institutions such as The Boys' Farm to deal with child-welfare cases as well as those pertaining to delinquents. To put these developments into context, we must first look at the child-welfare system in the Province of Quebec before 1950. This introduction presents the key features of the new 1950s' legislation against the backdrop of the growing provincial involvement in child-welfare matters. It also gives an historical overview of Montreal's Protestant social service agencies and child-welfare institutions.

CHILD-WELFARE POLICY IN
THE PROVINCE OF QUEBEC

Social welfare policy in the Province of Quebec[1] developed within the context of deference to private, Catholic, charitable institutions, on the one hand, and nationalist resistance to federal government intrusion, on the other. Initially, clerical control over health, education, and welfare institutions delayed and shaped provincial involvement; in 1921, however, the Province of Quebec intervened in these areas for the first time. Its goal was to help subsidize charitable institutions overburdened with increasingly urgent demands for their services, particularly in Montreal.[2] With its Public Charities Act (1921), which benefited existing Catholic institutions but generated a storm of controversy and clerical opposition to potential state interference and secularization, further reform was discouraged (Vigod 1979).[3] In fact, the Public Charities Act "served as the statutory basis of welfare organization in Quebec for forty years" (Vigod 1978, 167). In 1932, the act was extended: subsidies were provided not just for charitable institutions and institutional care, but for social service agencies ("institutions without walls") that assisted families in their own homes or placed children in foster homes.[4] For the next many years, the province helped to support, but did not otherwise regulate, a wide array of private charitable institutions and social service agencies, organized along religious and ethnic lines.

During the 1940s, the Province of Quebec put structures into place that eventually permitted increased provincial involvement in the area of child welfare. In 1943, with the death of several children from unsanitary conditions in commercial nurseries, a provincial royal commission was convened on nurseries and the general welfare of children. This Garneau Commission recommended the institution of separate provincial departments dealing with health[5] and social welfare, family courts, and individualized assessment; it also suggested foster home and institutional placements be given equal emphasis (Mongeau 1967, 71). Several child-welfare reforms resulted: the Child Protection Act (1944) was drawn up, but not implemented under the succeeding Duplessis government; the first provincial Department of Social Welfare – which became the Department of Social Welfare and Youth[6] under Duplessis in 1946 – was established; and a Child Aid Clinic was put in place to provide psychiatric and psychological assessments in delinquency cases for judges at Montreal's juvenile court.[7] Finally, in 1950, new provincial legislation established social welfare courts (the renamed juvenile courts were given a somewhat broader mandate over family relations)[8] as well as youth protection schools.

The Youth Protection Schools Act (1950),[9] redefined industrial and reform schools, giving them provincial contracts to accept court placements as "youth-protection schools"; it also gave the provincial Department of Social Welfare and Youth authority to place children in youth-protection schools on recommendation from the social-welfare court judges. The department allowed its placement authority to remain dormant,[10] however, leaving social-welfare court judges to place child-welfare cases in youth-protection schools. Judicial placements were limited, however, to those institutions with a provincial contract as a youth-protection school, that is, for those agreeing to receive court-committed protection cases in exchange for financial support on a per diem basis from the province. Provincial reform schools and industrial schools had already made such contracts; after 1950, therefore, they could receive neglected as well as delinquent clients. In other words, "protection cases" committed by the social-welfare courts under section 15 of the provincial Youth Protection Schools Act could be admitted, as could "delinquency cases" committed by the same courts under section 20 of the federal Juvenile Delinquents Act.

In the short run, the Department of Social Welfare and Youth did not act on the authority it had acquired – both to "classify" and "make general regulations for" youth-protection schools, and to place protection cases. But the legislation foreshadowed the province's growing involvement, particularly through its social welfare department, in child-welfare policy.

MONTREAL'S PROTESTANT CHILD-WELFARE INSTITUTIONS

Montreal's many private charitable institutions and social service agencies were grouped into four federations, organized along ethnic and religious lines: the Montreal Council of Social Agencies, the Federation of Jewish Philanthropies, the Federation of Catholic Charities, and the Fédération des oeuvres de charité canadiennes-françaises.[11] The first, the Montreal Council of Social Agencies, was formed in 1918 to link the city's anglophone, Protestant social-welfare agencies; its membership included four nineteenth-century orphanages which, in Montreal as elsewhere, constituted the first children's institutions.[12]

The Montreal Council of Social Agencies was set up to promote the new emphasis on family-centered, rather than institutional, care.[13] Not only did it help develop a foster-home placement agency, the Children's Bureau (1919), it was later to commission the Child Welfare League of America to survey its children's division (1924). As well, it lobbied the province to have financial support for charitable institutions extended to "non-institutional" foster-home placement agencies (1930),[14] and campaigned for measures to support poor families at home.

Initially, the new emphasis on foster-home placements appeared to support rather than threaten existing children's institutions. In the survey report that helped to found the Montreal Council of Social Agencies, John Howard Falk recommended that the "assignment of children to one institution or another should be left to an organization, with institutional facilities for temporary shelter, whose main functions would be (1) to make a thorough social, physical, and mental diagnosis of each child for whom admission to an institution is being sought, and (2) to keep an adequate record of every child passing through its hands" (Montreal Council of Social Agencies, Falk report, 1919, 31). With support from Montreal's private anglophone children's institutions, the Children's Bureau was thus formed to provide "a joint intake and investigation service to the institutions, and to find foster homes for an overflow group of children who could not be accommodated in the institutions" (MCSA, Report on Child Care, 1935, 6, 29). But dissension resulted when Carl Carstens, executive director of the Child Welfare League of America, in a survey some five years later, promoted foster homes rather than custodial care for normal children.[15] The dissension "fomented ... the serious difference of opinion around the respective values of institutional and foster home care";[16] and the "conflict between 'Foster Home' and 'Institution' protagonists" was to continue to plague the Montreal Council of Social Agencies' efforts to coordinate child care for many years. In an effort to placate institutions dissatisfied because of their vacancies for children, the Children's Bureau established a placement committee, "consisting of one delegate from each of the affiliated institutions," to determine the disposition of all applications "accepted for placement" (Montreal Council of Social Agencies, Report on Child Care and Protection, 1935, 21, 6). As the third section of this book will show, this early arrangement for accommodating the interests of institutions anticipated a strikingly similar "centralized" arrangement of the 1980s.

The activism of the Children's Bureau on behalf of foster-home placement, accelerated by the emergence of public relief for poor families, nonetheless threatened the existence of children's institutions by reducing their populations. By 1935, a new Montreal Council of Social Agencies survey reported that

the present institutional accommodation for children up to 14 years of age is greater than necessary ... Considerable difficulty has been experienced in filling these institutions during the last few years and though the institutions themselves lay the blame for this state of affairs at the door of the Children's Bureau, the Committee believes that it is partly the result of general conditions in the community and in particular of the institution of the system of government relief of the unemployed and their families, which has tended to keep together families that would otherwise have been broken up. (Montreal Council of Social Agencies 1935, 3, 5)

As a result, children's institutions reoriented their services toward foster home placement or amalgamated.[17] Thus, in 1950, when the Province of Quebec passed the Youth Protection Schools Act, Montreal's Protestant children's institutions included two surviving orphanages: Summerhill House, a small institution for girls up to the age of fourteen, and Weredale House, a "massive four-storey brown brick institution" designed to accommodate up to 180 boys between the ages of eleven to nineteen (Malarek 1984, 12). Located in the heart of Montreal, Weredale House provided a "highly regimented" routine for boys; the residents attended the nearby public school and were permitted to visit their families on Saturday afternoons (Caldwell 1967, 2).

Weredale House

Montreal's two private Protestant institutions for neglected and delinquent boys – Weredale House[18] and The Boys' Farm – viewed the new provincial Youth Protection Schools Act (1950) in terms of its potential for addressing their different client-recruitment problems. Under the new legislation, private children's institutions such as Weredale House could be designated as youth protection schools, by applying to the provincial Department of Social Welfare and Youth and agreeing to accept neglected youth committed by the Social Welfare Court in exchange for provincial financial support on a per diem basis. Weredale House used the threat of this option to free itself from dependence on the Protestant Children's Aid Society (as the Children's Bureau was now called) for clients.

To back track somewhat, Weredale House, in a centralized intake arrangement made in 1922, agreed to depend on the Protestant Children's Aid Society for referral of boys under the age of fourteen but to control its own intake of boys fourteen years and older.[19] Between the years 1922 and the early 1940s, when the average population at Weredale House increased from 75 to 145 (peaking at 159 in 1934), there were no serious problems (Weredale House Archives, Question of intake memorandum, 18 October 1950: 5, 2). By 1950, however, Weredale House faced a population crisis.[20] Its board of governors attributed the crisis not only to the Children's Aid Society's growing preference for non-institutional care (both in terms of efforts "to save the family for the child"[21] and foster home placement), but also to the closure of orphanages for young children that had served as primary "feeder institutions" for Weredale House via the Children's Aid Society.[22]

Declaring that "we have no intention of seeing Weredale House gradually close for lack of boys owing to our Intake arrangements being in the hands of an Agency which is not in sympathy with our work," the Weredale House board of governors threatened to change the institution into a provincial youth-protection school.[23] However, such a move would have deprived Protestant child-welfare agencies of their only remaining institution for boys; and it could also have invited unwelcome provincial involvement in response to the failure to present a united front.[24] The special committee set up by the Montreal Council of Social Agencies to mediate between Weredale House and the Children's Aid Society noted that "the recent enactment of provincial welfare legislation has very serious implications for the field both from a planning and financing standpoint," and recommended that "Weredale House assume responsibility for its total intake" (Weredale House Archives, correspondence on the question of intake, 6 February 1951).

Weredale House thus used the new legislation to free itself from dependence on the Children's Aid Society, thereby acquiring complete control over client recruitment. With freer and more direct access to young clients from a variety of referral sources, Weredale House no longer needed its classification as a youth-protection school to acquire clients. As a result, the new legislation did not directly affect Montreal's private Protestant children's institutions.[25] In effect, they chose not to contract with the province as youth-protection schools;[26] to do so would have meant losing their control over admissions to the Montreal Social Welfare Court.[27]

The Boys' Farm

The Boys' Farm viewed the new legislation from a different perspective. Under the Youth Protection Schools Act, both private reform schools and industrial schools (that had already contracted with the Province of Quebec to receive court-committed youth) were redefined as youth-protection schools. The Boys' Farm welcomed its new status as a youth-protection school, hoping to attract desirable youth protection cases in place of older delinquents. In a notice to staff members, Superintendent Evans announced:

On the 12th of October, The Boys' Farm and Training School received its license from Quebec to operate as a Youth Protection School. The establishment of

Youth Protection Schools has been undertaken in order to remove the "Reform School label" generally applied to Welfare and Training Institutions. It is important, then, for all of us to guard against the use of terms which in any way employ penal, criminal, or correction methods ... as the new legislation states clearly that these lads are sent to us for protection, to be educated and prepared for their eventual return to society (BFTS, internal correspondence, Evans, 27 October 1950).

The legislation seemed to promise a solution, in other words, to the long struggle with the Montreal Juvenile Court (now called the Social Welfare Court) over undesirable older clients. The Boys' Farm, however, as a publicly contracted youth-protection school and still dependent on the Montreal Social Welfare Court for the new type of client, now had to compete for desirable "protection" clients with Montreal's other Protestant child-welfare organizations, including Weredale House.

CHAPTER FOUR

Last-Resort Disposition of Protection Cases, 1950–1966

During the 1950s, Montreal's child-welfare organizations faced growing problems in the disposition of emotionally disturbed children – a reflection, in part, of the increased number of foster home placements. Not only were emotionally disturbed children difficult to place successfully in foster homes, but unsuccessful foster-home placements were only amplifying the problems of even normal children.

In 1953, the Children's Service Centre (as the Children's Aid Society was now called) expanded its temporary receiving facilities into a small separate institution, known as Allancroft,[1] for children whose behaviour and emotional disturbances made them difficult to place successfully in foster homes. A study of the 126 children admitted to Allancroft between 1953 and 1956 indicates that half of them were "neurotically disturbed," that more of Allancroft's disturbed children came from foster homes than from their own homes, and that half the children admitted to Allancroft from foster homes were there because of "the foster parent's inability to cope with the child's problem" (Chan et al 1957, 92).

But the study also provides evidence that foster-home placements frequently broke down for reasons that had nothing to do with the child's behaviour.[2] As a result, some children were placed in a sequence of foster homes. For example, the study's thirty-four children admitted to Allancroft from foster homes had already experienced ninety foster-home placements; their emotional disturbances were both the cause and the result of "too many placements" (Chan et al 1957, 95). From 1953 to 1956, Allancroft was used increasingly for older[3] "neurotically disturbed" children who had failed in foster-home placements; as a temporary placement facility,[4] it discharged these children to new foster homes or children's institutions which, in turn, exercised their own rights to select clients.

MONTREAL'S RESIDENTIAL
PSYCHIATRIC FACILITIES
FOR YOUTH

Residential psychiatric facilities for emotionally disturbed youth developed after 1958, when the Montreal Children's Hospital opened a psychiatric wing for children. The provision of free, publicly funded hospital care, after 1961, rapidly expanded these facilities. In 1962, there were residential psychiatric wards for children at three regular hospitals and other new wards were subsequently established at the Douglas Hospital, a hospital for patients with mental problems (in 1963, a wing was created for adolescent girls, followed, in 1965, by a wing for adolescent boys). Although child-welfare agencies sought placements for their emotionally disturbed clients in these new facilities, the hospitals controlled their admissions and, swamped by the high demand for all kinds of hospital care,[5] started to reserve residential psychiatric treatment for limited numbers of clients,[6] for specific periods of time.

In effect, psychiatric hospital wards not only failed to provide adequate placements for referrals from the child-welfare network, but themselves sought placements in child-welfare institutions for their discharged clients. For instance, when Summerhill House reopened in 1964, its group homes (for girls) were populated predominantly by clients referred from hospital psychiatric wards.

The selectivity of private child-welfare and psychiatric organizations meant that a growing number of emotionally disturbed children were being sent to youth-protection schools via the Montreal Social Welfare Court. Thus, after 1950, The Boys' Farm became a last resort – not only for older delinquents, but also for seriously disturbed boys rejected by foster homes, child-welfare agencies, children's institutions, and residential psychiatric facilities.

DEALING WITH
SERIOUSLY DISTURBED
YOUTH-PROTECTION CLIENTS

Seriously emotionally disturbed boys created severe problems at The Boys' Farm. Not only were they difficult to integrate into the school's program and daily life, and difficult to control, but the institute's efforts to arrange psychiatric services from Montreal's mental health organizations produced minimal results. In 1956, however, a psychiatrist from the Mental Hygiene Institute[7] requested permission to conduct a six-week "experiment" to evaluate the effectiveness of the drug Largactil on the residents of one cottage – twenty-one boys between eight and eleven years of age. Although the project was methodologically inadequate[8] and the results never reported, the practical benefits of the tranquillizer were immediately apparent. Two years later, the superintendent described the project to an interested reform-school superintendent in Ontario, concluding, "During the course of the project, there were no serious cases as the result of side effects, and our Cottage Parents and teachers were quickly aware of a 'quietening effect' and a general improvement in the behaviour of the group as a whole. We have since continued to use this medication in individual cases with satisfactory results" (BFTS, external correspondence, Evans, 8 November 1958).

Although the continued use of tranquillizers at The Boys' Farm after 1956 alleviated some of the problems of dealing with the emotionally disturbed youth committed by the Montreal Social Welfare Court – problems shared, incidentally, by Montreal's other youth-protection schools – it did not rectify the situation.

Efforts to Control the Admission
of Disturbed Boys

In the early 1960s, The Boys' Farm and Montreal's francophone youth-protection schools began to send "inadmissible" protection cases back to the Montreal Social Welfare Court and its detention facility. Unlike delinquency cases, protection cases could be legally committed to youth-protection schools by the provincial Department of Social Welfare and Youth on the recommendation, but not direct authority, of social-welfare court judges. By sending emotionally disturbed protection clients back to the court, the youth-protection schools therefore hoped not only to activate the dormant authority of the provincial welfare department,[9] but also to invoke the section of the Youth Protection Schools Act that read: "Directors (of Youth Protection Schools) are not obliged to receive or keep children whose physical or mental condition prevents them from conforming to the regulations of the School" (Quebec 1950, Youth Protection Schools Act, III.11).

In 1960, The Boys' Farm's board of directors adopted a new admissions policy, agreeing to accept protection-case boys conditionally and only after "careful consideration of social and medical history and on the understanding *that after a three month trial, if the case does not respond to treatment, the Courts will be requested to make other dispositions of the case"* (BFTS, administration committee minutes, 12 January 1960; emphasis in original). Acting on its new admissions policy, The Boys' Farm began to refuse boys committed without documents, and to return boys to the Montreal Social Welfare Court if they proved unsatisfactory after a three-month trial. In reaction, the judges insisted on their legal authority to place protection cases; in June 1962, Judge Long wrote to the president of the board of directors of The Boys' Farm, saying, "I have been given to understand that the Farm has been recognized as a Youth Protection School and, as such, has entered into a contract with the Minister. Section 10 of the Act respecting Youth Protection Schools states, 'The Director *shall receive and keep* all the children entrusted to him pursuant to this Act'" (BFTS, external correspondence, Long, 13 June 1962; emphasis in original).

The efforts of Montreal's youth-protection schools to control the commitment of disturbed youth-protection cases meant that increasing numbers of "inadmissible children" were being returned to the Montreal Social Welfare Court's detention facility. The case of "Ralph Kirby" will serve as an illustration. Ralph, who had been referred to the St-Jerome Social Welfare Court by a children's institution outside Montreal, was committed to The Boys' Farm in 1958 as a protection case "for an indefinite period." Five years later, the assistant superintendent of The Boys' Farm described Ralph's situation to the judge who had committed him:

Ralph's adjustment was slow and not without difficulties due primarily to a low intelligence (I.Q. 67). This, combined with an emotional problem that necessitated medication, made it impossible to effectively integrate him into our academic program. However, with the passing of time and the boy's rapid physical development, it became increasingly necessary to make some definite plans for his future. With this in mind, the subject was discharged on a trial basis (in June 1963) ... A job placement was arranged by our Department of Rehabilitation which included living accommodation.

Toward the end of July it became apparent that Ralph could not be retained by his employer – a poultry farmer some miles north of Shawbridge – since the boy had been discovered choking chickens to death "because their noise bothered him and it made him feel better after he had killed them." Consequently Ralph was removed from his employment and placed in detention at the Montreal Social Welfare Court, where he is at present time. (BFTS, external correspondence, Riddington, 17 October 1963)

In 1964, in response to complaints from Montreal Social Welfare Court judges, the provincial Department of Family and Social Welfare began to activate its dormant legal authority regarding the disposition of youth-protection cases. On the one hand, it set up a committee to examine the problem of "marginal cases"; on the other, it also issued a directive that youth-protection schools were not to refuse court-committed cases. This left The Boys' Farm to handle the continued commitment of seriously disturbed boys with tranquillizers and a weekly, half-day psychiatrist's visit from the Mental Hygiene Institute. In 1964, the superintendent regarded the boys "requiring psychiatric assistance" as his "greatest problem" (BFTS, administration committee minutes, 13 April 1964).

THE FIRST EXTERNAL SURVEY AT THE BOYS' FARM

To deal with these seriously disturbed boys, the board of directors of The Boys' Farm commissioned the first external survey in the institution's long history. The board sought the professional advice of psychiatric experts from Montreal's emerging children's mental-health network, as well as contacts that would generate practical support for disturbed clients – whether in the form of psychiatric services or alternative placements. Dr Hyman Caplan, assistant director of psychiatry at the Montreal Children's Hospital, was hired to carry out the survey.[10] The resulting Caplan report (BFTS, reports, February 1966) was supplemented with a report from Dr Marcilio, a psychiatric intern from the Montreal Children's Hospital who carried out his research while living at The Boys' Farm during December 1965.

Dr Marcilio's confidential seventeen-page report to the board of directors was candid and highly critical. In a description of what boys learned about The Boys' Farm before arriving (during their "three weeks to six months" spent in the court's detention centre where they encountered runaways from The Boys' Farm), Dr Marcilio noted that the boys learn "that it is a place where the older boy beats the younger, the stronger beats the weaker and where nothing is done about it.[11] [They learn] that it is very dangerous to be a 'stoolie' ... also that it is a place from where it is very easy to run away." As for the cottage parents who staffed the six cottages, Dr Marcilio observed:

The Boys' Farm is extremely short of professional staff. Almost all the staff live on the Farm and it seems that the Superintendent has more of a problem with them than with the boys committed to the Institution. Some of the staff have been living in the Institution for a good many years and many are only job-holders ... As it is extremely difficult to get staff for Shawbridge often the Institution has to take the first applicant ... Very often one cottage parent tells you that he has no problems with the boys and knows how to handle them. One couple who had been at the institution for one year said, "I don't push them around and I don't let them push me. If a boy comes to me and wants to tell me his problems I tell him to keep his troubles to himself, I have enough of my own. If he makes a fuss I tell him that he is the one who broke the law, not me." (BFTS, reports, Marcilio report, February 1966)

Although his report was "destructive in order to be eventually constructive," Dr Marcilio's inside knowledge of conditions at The Boys' Farm was to have an unexpected impact on future court commitments. In 1966, when Dr Marcilio completed his internship and went to work for the new Child and Family Clinic, he used his inside knowledge of the Farm to recommend against placements there.

DEVELOPMENT OF THE CHILD AND FAMILY CLINIC[12]

In 1966, an enterprising psychiatrist, Dr Shamsie, seized the initiative of coordinating children's services in alliance with the Montreal Social Welfare Court. As director of adolescent services at the Douglas Hospital (a psychiatric hospital), Dr Shamsie established a Child and Family Clinic, designed to assess anglophone children for the Montreal Social Welfare Court[13] and to make recommendations regarding their disposition. The clinic was intended "to act as a coordinating influence for the Agencies serving children coming from the Court" (Douglas Hospital Annual Report, 1966, 131). To this end, Dr Shamsie held joint meetings with representatives from correctional and protective institutions for children[14] "to interpret the purpose and function of the Clinic to these agencies, to learn from each its function, admissions policy and service limitations, and to identify missing services indicating a community need" (Summerhill Homes Archives, Social Welfare Court Child and Family Clinic, May 1966).

The operation of the Child and Family Clinic, financed by the provincial Department of Health, signalled the emergence of psychiatric professionals as influential arbiters in the disposition of anglophone delinquent and neglected youth. From 1966 through 1968, the court was to refer between 400 and 500 cases a year for assessment.[15]

CRISIS AT THE BOYS' FARM

The operation of the Child and Family Clinic had an immediate effect on The Boys' Farm. Initially, judges at the Montreal Social Welfare Court hoped to use the clinic's recommendations to counter the attempts of The Boys' Farm to refuse boys on the grounds of their unfit mental condition.[16] They actually did so in a few cases. As it turned out, however, the clinic more commonly recommended against placements at The Boys' Farm. The clinic's psychiatric professionals' inside knowledge of conditions at the institution (via Dr Marcilio) thus contributed to a serious drop in the population of The Boys' Farm in 1966. For example, by January 1967, the number of youth-protection cases at The Boys' Farm had dropped to forty-one, from eighty-one in January 1965 (BFTS, reports, Shamsie report, 1967).

At the end of 1966, The Boys' Farm was a dying institution. Not only had its resistance to the commitment of older delinquents and emotionally disturbed protection cases alienated judges at the Montreal Social Welfare Court, but its attempts to get help from Montreal's mental health network had backfired as well. Professionals, learning of the Farm's inadequate facilities and lack of professional staff, used their new influence over court dispositions to refer boys elsewhere.[17] By this time, the Farm's average population had dropped to ninety-six boys, the lowest level since its opening years. The Farm's continued existence was placed in doubt – not just because court commitments had fallen so low, but also because the institution depended for revenue on the per diem subsidy it received from the Province of Quebec for each court-committed boy. It was almost out of boys, and almost broke.[18]

THE SHORTAGE OF FOSTER HOMES

Montreal's anglophone children's institutions, however, were flourishing, primarily because of the shortage of foster homes. In 1965, the shortage was so serious that the anglophone Protestant, Catholic, and Jewish child-welfare organizations[19] launched a joint experiment to recruit 1,500 new foster homes for anglophone children. In 1966, the Children's Service Centre reported that the "dearth of foster homes was alarming" (Montreal Council of Social Agencies, *Red Feather Year Book*, 1966).

The shortage of foster homes expanded the populations of the children's institutions, enhancing their ability to select more so-called normal clients, particularly adolescents, thus allowing them to forestall transformation into "respecialized" (Rooke and Schnell 1983) facilities for problem clients.[20] Indeed, the population of Weredale House, so threatened by foster-home placements in the late 1940s, recorded a series of population highs between 1965 and 1967.[21]

The shortage of foster homes also enhanced the popularity of group homes as an acceptable – but expensive[22] – compromise between foster homes and child-welfare institutions. Between 1964 and 1966, Summerhill established three group homes[23] (including one for young boys) and planned to open another for boys "around twelve," thus encroaching on the client population long served only by Weredale House.[24] When consulted on the matter by Summerhill's board of directors,[25] the president of the board of directors of Weredale House declined to meet: "I question the need for Summerhill House to embark upon a program, at this time, for the care of boys over 12 years of age as we know of no occasion upon which we have refused requests from either the court or a recognized social agency to accept a boy in our age group, 10 to 18 years old, unless it was clearly evident to the members of our staff that the agency to be considered was the Boys' Farm" (Weredale House Archives, 14 November 1966).

CONTROL OF CHILD-WELFARE ADMISSIONS

The history of The Boys' Farm from 1950 to 1966 illustrates the unintentional impact of legislation intended to extend a measure of public control over the disposition of neglected youth, and calls attention to two issues. The first was the disarray created in the child-welfare network by the differential control over admissions of private organizations with and without public contracts, as well as the increasingly obvious need for coordination in the disposition of problem youth. The second was the high cost of organizational resistance which – in the case of The Boys' Farm – demonstrated not only the authority of the court over private institutions with public contracts, but also the emergence of psychiatric professionals as influential arbiters in the disposition of neglected, emotionally disturbed, and delinquent youth.

Control of Admissions in Child-Welfare Organizations

Between 1950 and 1966, the politics of client recruitment began to knit together the organizations of Montreal's Protestant child-welfare and mental health networks into an increasingly interdependent unit. The groups interacted more often, in their efforts to select desirable clients and to seek scarce placements for the emotionally disturbed and adolescent youths who could not be placed in foster homes. Cooperative strategies to coordinate the disposition of clients, however, remained undeveloped. During this same period, although the Montreal Council of Social Agencies made many efforts to coordinate the services of member agencies, the implementation of council recommendations was to remain in the hands of the private organizations, whose boards of directors acted to preserve their organizational autonomy, particularly in matters affecting client recruitment. The long-simmering tension between child-welfare agencies and children's institutions was eased, primarily because of the shortage of foster homes; children's institutions could then refuse undesirable clients without adversely affecting the size or composition of their client populations. The selectivity of private child-welfare and mental health organizations and their lack of coordination meant that difficult clients were "dumped" on the social welfare courts. This only underscored the court's lack of authority over the private child-welfare and mental health networks and, therefore, over the disposition of child-welfare cases.

In 1965, Canada's Department of Justice Committee on Juvenile Delinquency documented the problems posed by selective intake on the part of private organizations, for Canadian juvenile court judges and for reform schools more generally. Regarding the selective intake of child-welfare agencies, their report observed: "There is a serious shortage of foster homes, at least in the urban areas of Canada. It is no reflection on the private agencies when it is said that they have used their 'right' of selective intake to concentrate increasingly not only on younger children but on those whom they feel will benefit most by their services. In practice this has meant acceptance of children whose families give promise of cooperation through financial support" (Canada 1965, 177). The report commented, as well, on the selective intake of hospitals:

In many cases children who should be sent to hospitals with in-patient facilities for treatment of the mentally ill or to other specialized residential treatment centres are sent instead to training schools. The reason for this unhappy practice seems to be that hospitals and other treatment institutions control intake ... We are told that there is considerable reluctance on the part of hospitals to accept children requiring psychiatric care on an in-patient basis. On the other hand, superintendents of training schools have no control over intake. A child who is committed to such a school must be admitted even if there is no bed available for him. Only a few of the large metropolitan areas have residential centres for emotionally disturbed children and these, it would appear, also have very restrictive intake policies. (Canada 1965, 184)

In Montreal, as elsewhere, the court's limited jurisdiction meant that troubled young clients were sent to reform schools, thus increasing and altering the composition of reform-school populations.

Costs of Organizational Resistance

After 1950, The Boys' Farm – like training schools elsewhere – became the court's last resort, not only for older delinquents, but also for seriously disturbed boys rejected by foster homes, children's institutions, child-welfare agencies, and hospital psychiatric services. The board of directors of The Boys' Farm tried hard to resist these consequences. Its strategies – strategies that tried to control client recruitment by focusing on the court as well as the mental health network – backfired however, severely reducing its client population and threatening its very survival.[26] In effect, the creation of a court assessment-clinic that combined the authority of the court with the views of the professionals it had consulted cost The Boys' Farm dearly.

Between 1950 and 1966, The Boys' Farm nevertheless began to operate in a wider interorganizational context, one that included new contacts with Montreal's mental health and child-welfare networks as well as advice from external and professional experts. The pay-off came when broader developments brought new public funds and public intervention into the private sector.

CHAPTER FIVE

Threat of Provincial Intervention

After 1965, political and economic developments at the provincial and federal levels began to alter the environment within which private social service organizations of the Province of Quebec operated; these developments also produced increasingly explicit interorganizational activity within the anglophone social service network of Montreal. Acting both collectively and individually, child-welfare agencies and institutions sought external expert advice from professionals that would enable them to anticipate provincial intervention. This chapter introduces these developments within the context of the Province of Quebec's "Quiet Revolution," describing the efforts of the Montreal Council of Social Agencies to forge a collective response to potential intervention, and documenting the new strategies developed by The Boys' Farm to acquire control over admissions and to realign its position *vis-a-vis* the child-welfare network.

THE QUIET REVOLUTION

Constitutional arrangements in Canada allocate to the provinces the right to legislate health and welfare policy; nevertheless, the federal government has shaped provincial policies by providing cost-shared financing for federally defined programs. Prior to 1960, the Province of Quebec refused available federal grants in order both to preserve its distance from the federal government and to maintain the traditional character of private, Catholic educational and social welfare institutions – including orphanages, reform schools, and industrial schools. This policy of defensive nationalism was especially pronounced during the long regime of Maurice Duplessis (1936–39, 1944–59).[1]

With the election of Jean Lesage in 1960, the Province of Quebec began its "Quiet Revolution," a movement animated by a new and more aggressive form of nationalism[2] that produced innovative arrangements between the provincial and federal governments. In 1963, the Boucher report[3] "marked a turning point in the orientation of the Quebec government" toward both the federal government and the province's private social welfare agencies (Lesemann 1984, 51). Strongly advocating Quebec's need for an integrated economic and social policy, the report "stressed the importance of winning back the initiative in certain fields of jurisdiction from the federal government," and recommended that the province establish administrative control over private social agencies through full financing[4] (Lesemann 1984, 51–2).

The Province of Quebec no longer simply refused federal funds; it demanded, instead, the transfer of federally funded programs to the province. The ensuing conflict between the federal and provincial governments was partially resolved in 1964 when Quebec acquired the right to social service programs and funds (Coleman 1984, 136).[5] In July 1966, the Canada Assistance Plan authorized federal contributions toward half the cost of provincial welfare services, including the costs of care for children in welfare institutions; this vastly expanded the impact of Quebec's 1964 financial arrangements with the federal government. Yet under the terms of the Canada Assistance Plan (1966), cost-shared support for provincial welfare departments specifically excluded correctional services. As a result, "most of the provinces have redefined their treatment services for children so as to present a 'child welfare' rather than a 'child correction' orientation," thereby attracting additional federal support (Osborne 1979, 21).[6]

FIRST STEPS TOWARD PROVINCIAL INTERVENTION

In 1966, the Quebec government became active in the transformation of social welfare organizations. In February 1966, provincial officials from the Department of Family and Social Welfare began to meet jointly with representatives from Montreal's anglophone child-welfare agencies and institutions to review existing resources and needs. To induce private social service organizations to agree to the reduction of their autonomy, the province could now afford to offer the lure of full public-financing, on the one hand, and the implicit threat of withdrawn public funds, on the other.

Private welfare organizations were financed through a combination of mechanisms: provincial funds from the Quebec Public Charities Act; annual grants from interorganizational federations that sponsored joint fund-raising campaigns; and private endowments. Increasingly, inadequate public funding was producing higher organizational deficits;[7] these inadequate rates were "frozen" at their current levels in 1966, pending government review. The lure of full public-financing was further enhanced by the initiation of public salary scales, thereby raising staff salaries long suppressed by the poverty of many private organizations and expanding budgets to permit the hiring of professional staff. During 1966, three of the anglophone social service organizations of Montreal became parapublic agencies.[8]

RESPONSE OF THE MONTREAL COUNCIL OF SOCIAL AGENCIES

In the spring of 1966, these events began to shape interorganizational relations among Montreal's child-welfare organizations. The trigger was the Montreal Council of Social Agencies' convening of meetings, with the presidents and executive directors of the member child- and family-welfare organizations, to propose an external survey.[9] Although the council had long tried to coordinate the services of member agencies – often through the device of external surveys – it had faced the resistance of private organizations' boards of directors. The council now generated support for an external survey, despite continued resistance,[10] by invoking the threat of provincial intervention.[11]

In order to solicit support and interorganizational coordination for the survey, the council formed the Technical Advisory Committee, composed of board presidents and executive directors, representing participating agencies, as well as liaison representatives from the provincial government and two other Montreal federations.[12] Thus began, in February 1967, the National Study Service[13] survey.

By this time, the prospect of provincial intervention was even more evident. In late 1966, the Department of Family and Social Welfare and the Department of Health had appointed a joint commission to study the entire field of health and social welfare in Quebec. In January 1967, the Montreal Council of Social Agencies notified member agencies that the Castonguay Commission was inviting briefs from social welfare organizations; the deadline was September 1967. The National Study Service surveys of individual agencies and its ensuing recommendations to the Montreal Council of Social Agencies shaped the two groups' respective briefs to the Castonguay Commission. The Castonguay Commission's five-year inquiry and voluminous Castonguay-Nepveu report (Quebec 1967–72) was to provide the blueprint for Quebec's massive reorganization of health and social services in 1971 (Quebec 1967–72).

These developments made the cooperative coordination of children's services imperative, if only to avoid the intervention and imposed coordination that obvious conflict would ensure.[14] In other words, presenting a united front to the province and the Castonguay Commission had its advantages. At the same time, however, these developments also provided child-welfare organizations with strong motives for enlisting the support of child-welfare experts, as well as the province, to preserve and strengthen the position of their own organizations, particularly regarding the issue of control over client recruitment.

THE BOYS' FARM

The board of directors of The Boys' Farm managed the threat of provincial intervention (and, as will be seen below, the Farm's serious population crisis) by carefully using external surveys, contacts with officials from the Department of Family and Social Welfare, and the expertise of new professionals. These strategies began to take shape in 1966.

Initially, when the Montreal Council of Social Agencies proposed its external survey in the spring of 1966, The Boys' Farm was still hoping to profit from its own Caplan-Marcilio survey. Therefore the board, although it expressed some apprehension about the Council survey, agreed to participate. By the fall, however, the board had identified the Child and Family Clinic – the screening clinic for the juvenile court – as the source of its deepening population troubles.[15] In a canny political move, it immediately engaged the clinic's director, Dr Shamsie, as an external expert "to investigate the reasons for the decrease in population over the last few years and also to define the role and the function of The Boys' Farm in the future" (BFTS, reports, Shamsie report 1967, 2). That Shamsie survey, begun in November 1966,[16] was completed in April 1967, just as the National Study Service, in accordance with the Montreal Council of Social Agencies survey, was sending its child-welfare expert, Richard Clendenen,[17] to begin its survey of The Boys' Farm.[18] Within a period of three years, The Boys' Farm was thus surveyed by external experts three times: twice by its own commissioned psychiatric experts and once by collectively commissioned child-welfare experts. By the time the collectively commissioned report was completed (Clendenen 1967a), the board of directors of The Boys' Farm had already begun to act on the recommendations made in the Shamsie report.

All three reports concluded that The Boys' Farm should not deal with emotionally disturbed boys nor with youth-protection cases, recommending that these be referred instead for probation, to Weredale House, or to the psychiatric sections of hospitals. The reports also recommended a new role for The Boys' Farm – a concentration on the *treatment of delinquents*. To that end, they recommended that the Farm hire professionally trained staff to supervise that treatment and create a small locked unit for boys temporarily out of control.

The board of directors of The Boys' Farm, who had favoured the commitment of protection cases since 1950, had been trying to accommodate emotionally disturbed boys so that the institution would not be transformed into a juvenile prison for older delinquents. The Shamsie report, however, caused the board to take steps in a seemingly different direction. First, the board adopted a new admissions policy, announced to provincial officials in the summer of 1967,[19] in which it agreed not only to deal solely with delinquents but also to create a locked unit at The Boys' Farm. The board informed Judge Long at the Montreal Social Welfare Court of its decision. Having thus temporarily pacified the court, which had long advocated a locked detention unit at The Boys' Farm, the board then lobbied the Department of Family and Social Welfare to persuade the court to send the protection cases elsewhere. Second, the board, having recruited a director of services – the professionally trained social worker, Ronald Wylie – to implement a treatment program for delinquent boys,[20] began to lobby the Department of Family and Social Welfare for funds to support this director and his program. By appearing to move toward turning The Boys' Farm into a partially locked reform school for delinquents, the board and its external experts laid the groundwork for acquiring control over admissions. That is, they framed these concessions to the court in the language of treatment, which was later used to justify institutional, rather than judicial, control over admissions.

Selective Admission of Delinquents

A selective admissions policy, one that would permit The Boys' Farm to refuse undesirable delinquents committed by judges at the Montreal Social Welfare Court, required both a compelling rationale and a mechanism for enforcing that rationale.

The Farm's new director of services supplied the rationale. Borrowing from work being done with delinquents in California, Wylie promoted and installed a "differential-treatment" program at The Boys' Farm. That is, delinquents committed to the institution went first to a locked intake, or diagnostic, unit in which, after undergoing an evaluation of their "interpersonal maturity level," they were classified as one of nine delinquent subtypes.[21] The boys were then assigned to a cottage where they were to receive the treatment appropriate for boys of their delinquent type. The differential-treatment program created a "child-welfare" rather than a "child-correction" profile for The Boys' Farm, and at a time when federal-provincial agreements facilitated the funding of such programs. The differential-treatment program therefore supplied a particularly salient rationale for requests to the Department of Family and Social Welfare for increased staff and facilities at The Boys' Farm. Wylie not only argued that, without such increases, only a limited number of boys could be treated in a single cottage, but also that the number of existing cottages limited the number of delinquent subtypes that could be treated. The differential-treatment program also supplied a rationale for selective admissions that laymen, notably judges, could not easily dispute.

The Boys' Farm administrators were on the lookout for ways to subordinate the authority of judges at the Montreal Social Welfare Court to the Farm's own desire for selectivity. The problem was that while the Department of Family and Social Welfare held the legal authority to place protection cases, social welfare court judges still held the legal authority to sentence and place delinquents. First, therefore, the administrators pushed for new legislation that would shift sentencing authority for delinquents from the social welfare court judges to the Department of Family and Social Welfare. The Clendenen report provided support for this argument, suggesting "that consideration be given to amending the law so as to permit the Social Welfare Court to commit delinquent children directly to the Department of Family and Social Welfare." Logically, it continued, the department might then establish a central reception and diagnostic centre to receive all such youngsters from the provincial juvenile courts. "This kind of development would greatly facilitate the sorting out or grouping of youngsters diagnostically for referral to most appropriate treatment resources" (Clendenen 1967a, 8).

Second, the administrators argued that both the judges and the Department of Family and Social Welfare had sentencing authority. Again, the Clendenen report had suggested this argument with its observation that, inasmuch as The Boys' Farm was a legally recognized youth-protection school, the minister had the legal right, according to the Youth Protection Schools Act, to classify youth-protection schools in such a way as to permit "a proper segregation of the children, taking into account their sex, age, religion and physical and intellectual development, and their antecedents" (Clendenen 1967a, 7).

In 1969, Wylie tested the matter of sentencing authority with Judge Long. The Boys' Farm had been delaying the admission of a number of court-committed boys on the grounds that its Diagnostic Intake Unit was full. In March, the frustrated Judge Long sent a client to The Boys' Farm without prior notification, hanging up the telephone when the Farm staff phoned to protest. When The Boys' Farm retaliated by depositing the boy in his office, Judge Long wrote a letter of protest to the chief judge at the Montreal Social Welfare Court. In his own letter to provincial officials about the incident, Wylie encouraged a confrontation between the Department of Family and Social Welfare and the Department of Justice, saying that, in all likelihood, this issue would have to be discussed with the Department of Justice and that "we feel that this meeting could best be initiated by yourself" (BFTS, external correspondence, Wylie, 24 March 1969).

With the support of the Department of Family and Social Welfare, The Boys' Farm successfully held its ground regarding its right to set the date of "admission for diagnosis." Writing to provincial officials again, three months later, Wylie acknowledged the court's resulting backlog of cases, but used this fact to stress the importance of treatment and the need for additional resources.

May we state that it is our intention to develop a cooperative working relationship with the Judges of the Juvenile Court based upon sound treatment programs for delinquent children. In view of the limited resources The Boys' Farm has had, we believe we have made every effort to assist the Judges with the placement of delinquent children. Judge Long is correct that we now have a waiting list of approximately two months but this is only because we do not have the necessary resources to meet the demands of the Courts ... We realize that Judge Long does not want The Boys' Farm to become a treatment institution or (to) run a treatment program but we cannot and will not accept this point of view. (BFTS, external correspondence, Wylie, 30 June 1969)

In October 1969, The Boys' Farm established a selective admissions policy. Its board of directors agreed to accept all English-speaking children from the ages of twelve through seventeen for diagnosis, but to select for long-term treatment only "those male delinquent and acting-out children" who would "benefit from its treatment methods" (BFTS, board minutes, 8 October 1969).

The transformation of The Boys' Farm, from a dying institution of last resort to a model treatment facility for delinquent boys, was accomplished using the newly salient expertise of psychiatric and child-welfare professionals,[22] as well as the political and financial support of the provincial Department of Family and Social Welfare. While the population at The Boys' Farm continued to decline (from approximately 96 in 1966, to 76 in 1970–71), provincial financial support rose from about $200 thousand in 1966 to more than $1 million in 1970. Thus The Boys' Farm managed not only to acquire control over client recruitment, but also to sever the direct link between its budget and the number of clients – a factor that had always, in the past, escalated a population crisis into one pertaining to finances.

Impact on Other Institutions

Developments at The Boys' Farm affected the populations of other institutions. The population at the Farm decreased after 1965, because of both its initial failure (psychiatric experts at the court-screening clinic referred fewer clients after the Caplan-Marcilio Report backfired) and its subsequent success in implementing selective admissions. The upshot was that difficult clients went elsewhere.

Between 1966 and 1967, referrals from the Montreal Social Welfare Court to Weredale House almost tripled, remaining high through 1970–71.[23] Weredale House continued to control its admissions, however. Moreover, between 1967 and 1968–69, the number of clients discharged by Weredale House back to the Montreal Social Welfare Court and other child-welfare organizations more than doubled, remaining high through 1970–71.[24]

Although some boys were being placed at Weredale House, Allancroft,[25] Summerhill House, or within hospital psychiatric wards, the organizational efforts to control admissions, amplified by controlled admissions in Montreal's francophone sector, meant that many clients were being sent to the Montreal Social Welfare Court's detention centre. In 1966, the detention centre, with an average daily population of 500, admitted 4,945 dependent and delinquent boys between the ages of six and nineteen years (Clendenen 1967b, 665).[26] The provincial Department of Family and Social Welfare grew increasingly concerned and, in 1967, it notified Montreal's youth-protection schools[27] of the crisis conditions at the detention centre: "Centre St-Vallier is presently facing a certain number of difficulties due to overpopulation, rather critical to be frank, and the staff members are on edge and overtired because of stressing work conditions … we will most probably call a meeting very shortly to look the whole situation over and find ways and means out of the mess" (BFTS, external correspondence, 11 May 1967).

The Boys' Farm's success at enforcing its new, selective admissions policy contributed to these problems. In 1970, the anglophone probation officers wrote to the director of probation service at the Montreal Social Welfare Court to protest:

We would like to draw your attention to a situation at present existing with regard to English-speaking juvenile delinquents in the Province of Quebec, which is making the proper disposition of cases of serious delinquency cases increasingly difficult and often impossible … This letter is concerned with the intake policy of (The Boys' Farm) … We are not qualified, nor do we intend to criticise in any way the specialized type of treatment program outlined above. The problem which concerns the English judges and probation officers at the Court is … that as a result of this specialized program the intake policy of The Boys' Farm has become extemely selective. Any delinquent boy who has been committed to The Boys' Farm by the Montreal Court, yet who does not fit into any of the nine groupings already described, is returned to our detention center after a few weeks in the institution's diagnostic cottage … The Boys' Farm now regards itself as a specialized treatment centre caring for *certain types* of delinquent boys, and not as a training school giving service to the community by caring for committed juveniles within a prescribed area … We have found nothing in the Canadian Juvenile Delinquents Act indicating that only delinquent children having certain personality characteristics shall be committed to training schools. (BFTS, external correspondence, 1 September 1970; emphasis in original)

Through the newly legitimate language of treatment, The Boys' Farm had acquired control over admissions, thereby tempering its dependence on the Montreal Social Welfare Court and, hence, its status as a correctional institution.

In 1970, the province rebuilt the Centre St-Vallier adjoining Centre Berthelet, expanding the facilities of both. Together, the court detention centre and the juvenile prison provided the Montreal Social Welfare Court and Montreal's youth-processing organizations with backup placement locales for the unmanageable youth rejected by organizations in the juvenile corrections, child-welfare, and mental health networks. For anglophone Montreal, St-Vallier and Centre Berthelet replaced The Boys' Farm as the system's last-resort facility.

As for The Boys' Farm, it joined Montreal's other children's institutions and child-welfare agencies within the newly developing, interorganizational, child-welfare network.

THE POLITICS OF CLIENT RECRUITMENT AT CHILDREN'S INSTITUTIONS

Like The Boys' Farm, Montreal's anglophone child-welfare organizations dealt with the threat of provincial intervention by acting collectively, trying meanwhile to protect their own interests. After the completion of the Montreal Council of Social Agencies survey in 1968, however, the pursuit of organizational interests occurred within an increasingly explicit interorganizational context. Meanwhile, although private child-welfare organizations continued to resist centralized planning, the surveys of 1966–68 were generating interorganizational consulting bodies that affected private organizational policy. During 1969 and 1970, for example, a Group Care Committee[28] met weekly, referring its recommendations back to the boards of directors of individual, private, children's institutions. The influence of expert advice from child-welfare professionals on emerging provincial policies, as well as the negotiations within the Group Care Committee, produced new agreements regarding the disposition of clients among existing organizations.

Much as The Boys' Farm had profited by acquiring control over admissions, Summerhill House was now profiting, in turn, from the enthusiasm of child-welfare experts for group homes; provincial funding was acquired for more group homes as a result. In 1967, with five group homes (including one for boys about twelve years of age), Summerhill had plans to expand to twenty. Indeed, with four or five applications for every empty bed, Summerhill House could select its clients.[29] In 1970, Summerhill's board of directors adopted a new admissions policy in which further referrals from hospital psychiatric wards were to be refused. In response to written notification of the new policy, the psychiatrist-in-chief of the Jewish General Hospital wrote to convey his "dismay and regret." After acknowledging Summerhill's right to establish its own policy, he added: "If a psychiatric case is any youngster admitted to a hospital prior to request for group-home placement, then we do them a great disservice by admitting them. Because, conceivably, were they to come to your attention through any other agency, with emotional problems, they would be acceptable. Under the circumstances I would like to register my protest" (Summerhill Homes Archives, 8 April 1970).[30]

Among the institutions serving boys, Weredale House – long the largest of Montreal's Protestant children's institutions – experienced the greatest difficulty in reconciling its traditional function with the views of child-welfare experts. In the late 1960s, its board of directors had to withdraw its refusal to open a diagnostic unit and to care for more disturbed boys.[31] As a result, under the guidance of the Group Care Committee, Weredale House was reluctantly transformed into a "respecialized" (Rooke and Schnell 1983) children's institution.

Intervention by provincial officials and interorganizational planning bodies both deferred to, and undercut, the traditional autonomy of private organizations. The resulting tension between public and private control over child-welfare policies is conveyed in the following letter from the Department of Family and Social Welfare's director of institutional resources to the Weredale House board of directors:

It is the privilege, and the duty of the Board to set its policies: the Group Care committee can recommend; the government state its preferences in keeping with needs or priorities; but the final decision of what services the institution is willing to render is the responsibility of the Board. Notwithstanding its shortcoming, the comparison to buyer and seller applied to Government and Board may illustrate to some extent the type of relationship and responsibilities implied. In the present case we do wish to buy from Weredale House treatment-oriented services for English-speaking adolescents. (Weredale House Archives, Minutes of the Board of Governors meetings, 15 February 1971)[32]

These developments heralded provincial reorganization of the health and welfare sector. In 1971, when the Act Respecting Health and Social Services consolidated the transformation of private organizations into para-public outfits, new parameters were established for interorganizational relations and the disposition of clients in the child-welfare network.

CONCLUSION

The history of The Boys' Farm from 1966 to 1971 provides information about the specific links between larger political and economic struggles, the expansion of the welfare state, the influence of treatment-oriented professionals, and the disposition of young clients.

Indeed, events at The Boys' Farm during the late 1960s illustrate the impact of the treatment-oriented professionals on emerging provincial policy. Psychiatric and child-welfare experts favoured a clinical, child-welfare orientation rather than a legal, correctional orientation toward problem youth. The clinical language of assessment, classification, and individualized treatment was persuasive, in part because it seemed to provide a compelling and enlightened approach to dealing with youth.

But this approach was also salient for other political and financial reasons. The Province of Quebec's new stance toward the federal government involved reclamation of its provincial right to control welfare. As well, the federal government's provision of new funds for provincial welfare departments, along with its stipulations as to their use, favoured the redefinition of correctional services. These developments combined to erode the authority of social welfare courts over the disposition of delinquent and dependent youth. In any event, the Province of Quebec did not intervene to shore up judicial authority; instead, it acted to expand the authority of the Department of Family and Social Welfare, child-welfare networks, and the social work professionals who staffed these networks. Thus, from 1971 to 1977, as we will show in the next section of the book, new provincial policies resulted in a shifting of authority over the disposition of delinquent and dependent children away from the court and its ancillary institutions, including court assessment clinics.[33] Juvenile-court judges and psychiatric professionals were replaced by child-welfare professionals as the central arbiters in the disposition of troubled youth.

PART THREE

A Mandated Youth-in-Trouble Network

Introduction

New Quebec legislation introduced during 1971 and 1977 radically altered the structures within which youth-processing organizations handled the disposition of delinquent, neglected, and emotionally disturbed youth. The combined legislation produced a "mandated youth-in-trouble network": that is a formal legalized network that operated according to a set of formally regulated procedures and interorganizational structures, and within which the disposition and institutional placement of troubled youth had to take place. This introduction reviews the major dimensions of these two pieces of legislation and outlines the resulting, reconstructed, anglophone youth-protection network of Montreal.

THE 1971 ACT RESPECTING HEALTH AND SOCIAL SERVICES

In 1971, the Province of Quebec acted on the work done by the Castonguay commission. The result was the Act Respecting Health Services and Social Services, legislation which extended public control over the province's many private and sectarian social service organizations, and divided the province into regions for the provision of health and social services, creating regional monopolies over these services.[1] The act also specified the functions of health and social service organizations, dictated the membership of their boards, and to some extent determined their interrelationships.[2]

The reorganized child-welfare network not only grouped social service agencies into regional "social service centres," but also redefined children's institutions, including youth protection schools, as regional "reception centres." Although, in spirit, the act favoured decentralization and client participation, the organizations created under its regulations were actually larger, more bureaucratized and more centralized than the organizations they replaced. Montreal's anglophone Ville Marie Social Services Centre, for example, was created through the merger of six, smaller, social service agencies. Reception centres also increased in size, particularly after the Batshaw committee's (1976)[3] recommendation that the "reception centre of the future" be "versatile" and provide a wide range of services.

The legislation shaped new structures for the placement of problem youth in institutions. Each reception centre, for instance, had to establish a cooperative admissions committee with the social service centre in its region, although the actual structure of these joint-admissions committees was left to the discretion of the organizations involved. Nevertheless the regulations of the act clearly favoured the authority of the social service centre in shaping these committees and, therefore, in controlling the disposition of troubled youth. For example, the ruling was that when the reception and social service centres could not agree on the structure of the joint-admissions committee, the social service centre should have the majority of members (Quebec 1981, section 78).

THE 1977 YOUTH PROTECTION ACT

By 1977, the provincial Youth Protection Act had further formalized the procedures affecting the disposition of problem youth and had completed the process of establishing direct governmental control over social services involving youth (Lesemann and Renaud 1980).

The act also created the position of a director of youth protection in each social service center; this official was to have wide responsibilities and authority over the welfare of the young people within the regional jurisdiction of the social service centre in question. The act permitted directors of youth protection to "delegate" their authority over individual cases to social workers at these centres and to the joint-admissions committees to which these "delegates" brought recommendations for the institutional placement of their clients.[4] The directors of youth protection were empowered, moreover, to order youth into reception centres and to monitor their programs through periodic written reports from delegates. Such authority was intended to ensure continuity of treatment and the protection of children's rights.

The Youth Protection Act was designed to keep all youth, including delinquents, from unnecessary contacts with the youth court.[5] Directors of youth protection were authorized to deal with the disposition of all problem youths by working out "voluntary measures," including institutional placement, with the youths and their parents. Court proceedings were reserved for cases in which "voluntary measures" could not be agreed to, and where "compulsory measures" were therefore necessary. Directors of youth protection thus acquired particular responsibility for protecting the rights of youths institutionalized via "voluntary measures," inasmuch as these placements were not reviewed by the youth court.

Together, these two pieces of legislation had particular ramifications for both the interrelationships between child-welfare agencies and children's institutions, and the issue of control over client admissions. The legislation gave the directors of youth protection at the social service centres effective control over the disposition of young clients, thus threatening the control over admissions that private children's institutions had enjoyed and were trying to maintain. At the same time, the Act Respecting Health and Social Services (1971) gave reception centres authority to define their admissions criteria and to refuse clients who did not qualify under those criteria (Quebec 1981, sections 75–6). As we will show in the following chapters, reception centres were able to use this contradiction to deal successfully with the threat to their autonomy introduced by the Youth Protection Act; indeed, they even benefited from its regulations.

MONTREAL'S ANGLOPHONE YOUTH-PROTECTION NETWORK

Montreal's anglophone youth-protection network includes the Ville Marie Social Services Centre[6] and two major reception centres. The Ville Marie Social Services Centre acts as the primary source of young clients for anglophone reception centres and psychiatric hospitals in Montreal.

Social Service Centre

The Ville Marie Social Services Centre comprises three area centres that serve clients within certain geographically defined locales; each is headed by a director who reports to the central executive director. Within that major social service centre[7] – it coordinates a wide range of social services – is a director of youth protection who is specifically responsible for child-welfare services. That official carries out this responsibility through the formal delegation of cases and authority to social workers in the three area centres, while heading a small department of several review analysts who monitor the work of these delegates.

Reception Centres

Two major reception centres fall within Montreal's anglophone youth-protection network; namely, Youth Horizons, and Shawbridge Youth Centres (formerly The Boys' Farm). Both provide a wide range of programs, including residential care, for adolescents between twelve and eighteen years of age.

Youth Horizons was formed in 1977 from an administrative merger of four children's institutions.[8] Like the institutions from which it evolved, Youth Horizons serves adolescents (and some preadolescents)[9] with mild emotional and behavioural problems, most of whom become residents under the "voluntary measures" provision of the Youth Protection Act. Its residential programs, located primarily in community group homes, vary widely in terms of degree of structure; two of its highly structured units incorporate classroom facilities.

Shawbridge Youth Centres, like the institution out of which it evolved, serves adolescents with more serious troubles: youths who are less manageable and more delinquent. Shawbridge provides a variety of residential services as well as programs – ranging from the locked, fenced, and highly structured units, through the more open cottage units at its original country site; to community group homes in Montreal. Shawbridge's institutional policy requires a court order as a condition for admission.[10] Adolescents whose behaviour improves, however, may sign a "voluntary measures" agreement, as they progress to the institution's more open programs.

Psychiatric Institutions

Psychiatric services and facilities are not formally included in the anglophone youth-protection network; they operate as part of a separate psychiatric network. Two anglophone psychiatric hospitals, however, do provide institutional care for youth, and one anglophone children's hospital has a psychiatric ward. Psychiatrists represent these institutions "informally" on the anglophone joint-admissions committee, recruiting and informally coordinating the admission of clients to their respective programs for youth.

Joint-Admissions Committees

Between 1978 and 1982, the anglophone youth-protection network experimented with three joint-admissions committee structures (centralized, decentralized, and recentralized), each being the product of voluntary agreements among the managements of the social service centre and the reception centres. Chapters 6 and 7 examine how these three structures affected the institutional placement of youth, as well as the interests of the organizational participants. Chapter 8 examines the ways in which the procedures, designed to protect the rights of institutionalized youth through periodic external review, were watered down in practice.

CHAPTER SIX

Centralized Disposition of Clients

From 1978 to 1981, decisions concerning the placement of Montreal's anglophone youth in reception centres were made by a centralized joint-admissions committee. That committee included representatives from the Ville Marie Social Services Centre (the representative from the department of youth protection served as committee chair), the anglophone reception centres, and the anglophone psychiatric hospitals.[1]

The demand for institutional placements for adolescents was invariably greater than the supply of available reception-centre "beds." Indeed, only the preadolescent programs had more available beds than clients. Although the availability of reception-centre beds fluctuated (principally because most clients "graduated" from these centres at school year-end), constraints on the deployment of available resources made it difficult to reconcile even this limited supply of beds with the existing demand. Reception centres, for example, were required to use their resources for the purposes funded by the government; without government approval, they could not even convert "institutional beds" to "group-home beds," should a greater demand for group-home placements occur.

The centralized structure provided a vehicle for a seemingly rational coordination of resources to fit client needs, particularly given the scarcity of these resources and the constraints on their use. In practice, however, the centralized committee provided institutions with a forum where client problems and needs could be redefined to suit the resources available.

THE CENTRALIZED COMMITTEE AT WORK

The centralized committee, which met once a week for two to three hours to review recommendations for institutional placement, usually processed four to six referrals a meeting. The recommendations came from the area-centre social workers, who worked directly with the clients for whom they had received formal youth-protection responsibility.[2] Incidentally, these recommendations would already have been reviewed within the area centres before being referred to the centralized committee.

The referring worker, accompanied by the area-centre supervisor, personally presented the cases to the committee. To present a case, the referring worker was required to supply the committee with written reports on the client: the referring worker's own psychosocial report on the client and family; a report from the client's school; a psychological assessment; and a medical assessment. Together these reports, which could range from fifteen to twenty-five pages, documented the need for institutional placement and recommended a particular form of placement (for example, placement in a group home). Before making a decision, committee members read these reports quickly (perhaps for five minutes), using them as a source for questions and comments.   .

Committee decisions took one of three forms: *postponement*, *placement* (whether in the recommended program or not), or *refusal*. Although they were often governed by practical constraints as to placement resources available, these decisions were typically justified in *clinical* rather than practical terms – a process that impugned the professional competence of the referring workers. Since most workers were well aware of the shortage of residential resources, realizing that the availability of a "bed" in a particular program was in some cases the most relevant consideration, the committee's use of clinical arguments was especially frustrating. Symbolically at least, it suggested that the referring workers could not be trusted to share the "secrets" that determined placement decisions. Moreover, as described more fully below, it prevented workers from fully participating in the kind of face-saving discourse that Pfohl (1978) observed in his study of decision making in psychiatric teams.

Postponement

Committee decisions were sometimes postponed, on the grounds that missing documents, or additional information, were necessary if clinically appropriate decisions were to be made. Unfortunately, these requests for additional information were often framed in ways that challenged the adequacy of the referring workers' reports. Committee members frequently commented, for example, on the quality of the referring workers' psychosocial reports in ways that seemed to evaluate the workers more than the clients. Moreover, the committee's comments, although they justified postponements, were also intended to "socialize" referring workers to the procedures and standards of the committee. In fact, requests for "further information" did not necessarily produce new information, but rather a more formal documentation of what the referring worker already knew.

In one case, for example, the committee postponed a decision by challenging the referring worker's view that foster homes were no longer a viable option for the client; the worker had to return two weeks later with a long list of the client's unsuccessful foster-home placements. As non-institutional placements, foster-home placements were handled by the social service centre and its social workers, rather than the reception centres; thus they were not the responsibility of either the reception centres[3] or the committee. For referring workers, however, the foster-home option had limited appeal as an alternative: not only had their clients already been placed unsuccessfully in foster homes, but the supply of foster homes willing to take adolescents was limited.

The clinical rhetoric used by the committee to justify postponements often masked more practical considerations. Operating with limited resources for placement, the committee often used postponement as a tactic to delay the deployment of resources. In an interview, the committee chair acknowledged that requests for additional information were being used to "buy time," whether in terms of bringing the referral to the committee or of making a placement decision. Referring workers, whose competence was called into question during this process, paid for this "bought time"; it was their own scarce time that was being spent to satisfy the committee's demands.

Placement

When the committee made a placement decision, the clients were not necessarily placed in the kinds of institutional programs recommended by referring workers. The reality was that clients were allocated according to unwritten rules that served to protect the institutions represented on the committee and their relations with one another, even at the expense of the client or referring worker. These unwritten rules involved (1) honouring each other's claims to clients, (2) "escalating" the placement of clients to fit the available resources, and (3) "attaching" clients to the first organizations to which they had been "placed."

Honouring each other's claims to clients. The organizations represented on the committee, in accordance with the most fundamental, unwritten committee rule, honoured each other's claims to particular clients. Even in the case of programs for preadolescents, where the number of empty beds available in more than one reception centre always exceeded the supply of suitable clients, reception-centre representatives did not fight over clients, settling instead for their "fair share of the market."

The committee operated on the understanding that there was no need to discuss a case once an organization's representative had expressed interest in the client. Thus statements such as "I'll take it," "He looks OK for me," or "I have a bed for him" ended the discussion. For example, a psychiatrist once complained that he did not have a copy of a specific client's report; however, as the referring worker got up to bring him the report, a reception centre representative announced she would take the client, whereupon the psychiatrist told the referring worker he no longer needed the report. In another example, a psychologist was signalled to cut short his enquiries about one client; a representative of one of the reception centres had said it would be taking the client. By honouring each other's claims to particular clients, the committee members did not actively engage in establishing a "fit" between the client's needs and existing programs; instead, they allowed the institutional representatives to define and select their own clients.

This unwritten rule could be justified as a form of interorganizational respect for each other's arenas of expertise. Indeed, the institutional programs available for adolescent clients did address different kinds of adolescent troubles (psychiatric problems, delinquency, or the milder behavioural consequences of abuse or neglect). Thus, when a committee member representing one of these programs expressed interest in a particular client, the committee could honour the claim as a form of deference to the representative's presumed expertise regarding particular problem populations.

Organizational claims were honoured, however, even when the placement was not the kind recommended by the client's referring worker, and, more rarely, even when a fellow expert objected. In one such case, a psychiatrist so firmly objected to the psychiatric hospitalization of a client that she insisted that her objection be stated in the minutes of the meeting. Her insistence failed to alter the committee's decision, however, and was interpreted not as concern for the client's best interests but as a "spill over" from other, unrelated conflicts among the psychiatrists on the committee.

Escalation.   If the program that suited the client's needs and problems was filled, the committee compromised by referring the client to a program even further removed from normal community life, thus escalating intervention in the client's life. For some clients, referral to the committee already constituted an escalation,[4] a compromise brought about by the shortage of foster homes for adolescents. Further escalation might mean referring the client to a "cottage" rather than a group home. In the extreme form, these escalating compromises produced what the Shawbridge representative called "bonuses," that is, because Shawbridge workers usually work with older, more difficult, and more delinquent clients than those typical of Youth Horizons, these clients who were originally recommended for placement at Youth Horizons, but were instead placed at Shawbridge, constitute "bonuses" for the Shawbridge workers.

Although all escalations affected clients, a distinction can be made between *vertical* and *horizontal* escalations. Vertical escalation involved placing a client in either a more structured program than the one recommended by the referring worker, or in a program for a population more delinquent than that of the client's current program. In other words, it meant placing the client in a more "intensive" setting. Thus, the placement of a client in a Youth Horizons cottage rather than a Youth Horizons group home, when a group home had been recommended, would constitute "vertical escalation." In contrast, horizontal escalation involved placing a client in an institution that dealt with qualitatively different problems from the ones initially defined as the client's by the referring worker. Thus, the placement of a mildly delinquent client in a psychiatric hospital, when placement at Youth Horizons had been recommended, would constitute "horizontal escalation."

As in the case of the postponement decision, the practical considerations for escalation were usually masked by clinical rhetoric. The committee justified vertical escalation by redefining client problems in quantitative terms. Indeed, by redefining the client's behaviour as "more serious" than originally thought, the committee members and referring worker could agree that a more intensified placement was appropriate. Horizontal escalation, however, involved a more massive redefinition of the client's problems in qualitative terms. As one supervisor put it: "A reception centre is a reception centre, but a psychiatric hospital is a different story altogether." Horizontal escalations were, therefore, less common and less acceptable than vertical escalations. Nevertheless, although the vertical escalations were more acceptable than the horizontal to those making placement decisions, the former still affected the clients' lives.

The vertical escalation of clients took place not only within the context of the centralized committee, but also within the reception centres themselves, where the internal mobility of clients from one program to another constituted a form of vertical escalation. This internal vertical mobility was not easily scrutinized by outsiders. Nor were the patterns of client escalation from Youth Horizons to Shawbridge clear, even though a misleading impression of external scrutiny had been created by Shawbridge's policy of requiring a court order for client admission. Indeed, because the youth court had no authority to define the specific reception centre in which a client was to be placed, a "court order for placement in a reception centre" could be obtained without the reception centre being mentioned by name. The court was not in a position, therefore, to screen out cases of vertical escalation; thus these so-called bonuses found their way from Youth Horizons to Shawbridge.

This policy meant that adolescents were being sent to youth court for "compulsory" rather than "voluntary" placement, even when all parties (the youth, parents, and the director of youth protection) had agreed to the placement. The policy thus violated the intention of the Youth Protection Act to divert youth from court and to give placement authority over voluntary cases to the directors of youth protection. Unfortunately, not only did the policy send escalated clients to youth court, it also stamped them as the type of adolescent for whom a "compulsory" court-ordered placement was necessary.

Being court-ordered to a reception centre was, for clients, the end of their voluntary relationship to professionals. Even more importantly, clients were often not prepared for this step, because it was not what their social worker had led them to expect (nor what their social worker had recommended to the committee). In this respect, it is noteworthy that one referring worker was less disturbed about a client's vertically escalated placement at Shawbridge than about having to explain to the client and his family that they had to go to court to implement the placement.

Attachment.   Organizational claims regarding clients at the centralized committee were honoured as permanent claims, even when placements involved escalation. Shawbridge would not, for example, transfer bonus clients to Youth Horizons once the latter organization had an opening. In this sense, clients were "attached" to the organization that picked them up at the joint-admissions committee stage. This unwritten rule allowed the organizations to realize the benefits of escalation: it allowed them to keep the "good clients" recently acquired through escalation, and it also reduced their costs. In effect, it was less costly to retain old clients than to replace them with new ones, given the intensive use of organizational resources for assessment and socialization that occurred during the initial period of institutional placement.

The attachment principle provided the institutions with other benefits as well. It helped to keep them running at more or less steady and full capacity, a useful argument when justifications regarding demands to the government for additional beds had to be made. It also helped organizations to maintain their claims as to their respective domains within the youth-in-trouble network. Frequent transfers of clients across organizational boundaries might, in this sense, have diffused organizational claims to particular kinds of problem youth. The practice of escalation did, of course, mute clear distinctions among the client populations of institutions within the network (for example, mildly troublesome youth were sent to institutions for delinquent offenders, and "mild" delinquents went to psychiatric hospitals). But, again, this overlap was masked by clinical rhetoric that justified placement decisions as an appropriate match between (redefined) client needs and organizational services.

Finally, the attachment principle handled certain problems of mutual distrust that might otherwise have arisen. For example, if organizations accepted clients on a temporary basis pending a more appropriate opening elsewhere, they would have had to trust one another not only to release but also to accept the clients involved.[5] In this situation, organizations were likely to worry about failing to acquire promised clients, not to mention getting stuck with clients who turned out to be difficult.

Completion of the Placement Process

Once the committee had made a placement decision, the written reports on the client were given to the representative from the reception centre or psychiatric hospital selected for placement. The referring worker was asked to contact the representative to complete the placement. If the placement was at Shawbridge, the referring worker was also asked to obtain a court order if one had not already been issued. The psychiatrists and representatives from Youth Horizons were always careful to point out that they were accepting the case initially "for assessment"; the Shawbridge representative did not make this point quite so systematically. But all the committee placement decisions were recorded in the minutes as "recommendations for assessment in (name of institution)," thereby acknowledging and emphasizing the rights of institutions to screen clients for admission. Although the recommendations sometimes also specified the targeted program within the reception centre, the placement of clients in specific programs was, for the most part, left to the discretion of the reception centre. As we have noted, this issue had ramifications for clients who could be transferred easily across the wide range of programs run by Youth Horizons and Shawbridge.

Refusal

The committee, equipped with resources inadequate to the demand from referring workers for placement, could also refuse placements. But again its decisions were justified on clinical rather than practical grounds.

The committee most commonly justified such refusals by impugning the referring worker's familiarity with institutional services and, hence, their appropriate clinical use for particular clients. Because referring workers (and others who supplied the reports recommending placement) were more familiar with non-institutional services than with the variety and particularities of specific institutional programs, this tactic was effective. The committee used this tactic, for example, to challenge the placement recommendations made in reports from psychiatrists. When one referring worker said, for instance, that "the psychiatrist also recommended a group home," the committee chair asked another committee member (a psychiatrist), "Do psychiatrists know about our problems of limited group homes?" The reply was, "I am not sure they know what a group home *is*, never mind the availability of group homes." This tactic disqualified outsiders (including referring workers) from judging the kinds of services offered by reception centres and, therefore, their appropriate clinical use. Disqualification was a useful tactic – not only for justifying refusals, but also for preparing the referring worker to consider alternate, and escalating, forms of placement.

The committee also justified refusing referrals for institutional placement on clinical grounds, by implying that less intrusive, non-institutional approaches are more appropriate and should be tried first. In one case in which placement in a group home was sought for an abused foster child who had had no behavioural problems but was unwanted by his natural parents, the committee proposed that the referring worker get a court order to compel the family's participation in therapy (refusal of placement), or place the child in a psychiatric institution for assessment (a horizontally escalated placement). In this case, the referring worker and supervisor put up unusual resistance to the committee's clinically rendered advice: "I don't see why we have to go to court … We are talking about a child in danger … He is not a psychiatric case and he is not going to a

hospital ... Before we came here, we consulted our placement committee. We have supervisors, program coordinators, and altogether
ten professionals who sit on this placement committee. I do not need
your advice on this case. You either say yes or no. If you say no, we
will go back to our placement committee."[6] This resistance permitted
the committee's practical considerations to surface; at the conclusion
of the discussion the committee chair conceded that, although the
client should be placed in a group home, no room was available. The
supervisor replied, "OK, that's all we want to hear, that you are going
to take him but we will have to wait for a while."[7]

Although the committee sometimes proposed specific, alternative
clinical solutions to justify refusal (as in the initial suggestion for a
court order already discussed), it more often gave vague advice. For
example, "more family support" might be suggested. Refusals, as
was the case with postponements, often served to "buy time" for the
committee. In one such case, the referring worker was sent to
research community resources even though, as one committee
member said, "We know he will be back here in two weeks."

Use and Impact of Clinical Rhetoric

Because the diagnosis of client problems and the prognosis for various forms of treatment have been notoriously open to differences of
interpretation, the justification of committee decisions in clinical
terms was not difficult. Yet the committee's clinical assertions were
made about clients that committee members knew only from written
reports, produced by referring workers who knew these clients personally. Inasmuch as committee decisions often meant departures
from the recommendations of referring workers, the process of justifying these departures meant an attack on the referring workers'
clinical judgment: therefore the adequacy of the workers' reports and
case presentations was impugned; placements were escalated by
redefining the clients' problems and needs; and placements were
refused by questioning the workers' assessment of client problems
and their recommended solutions.

Although the "logic of justification and reconciliation" employed
by committee members and referring workers was similar to that
used by psychiatric teams in determining dangerousness (Pfohl
1978), several noteworthy differences should be mentioned. They
relate, first and foremost, to the partial participation of referring
workers in the process and, second, to the outcome of the delibera-
tions. As in Pfohl's study, the committee members selectively used
written reports to highlight the problems and needs that reinforced

and justified what they had already decided; unlike the teams he studied, however, not everyone contributed equally to the process of justification. For example, the referring workers did not necessarily realize where the committee members wanted to place the client until late in the discussion, when they were able to decipher the cues and figure out the target placement. This delay in participation was not critical when the "justification" was for the placement they requested. However, in the case of escalation, when "reconciliation" was required, early participation was more important; it would allow the workers to "save face" by accounting for any discrepancies between their recommendations and the decision of the committee. When no placement was approved, workers were doubly frustrated: by the outcome, and by the lack of opportunity to save face.

Under these circumstances, it is not surprising that referring workers termed their experiences with the centralized committee intimidating, even humiliating. What is more surprising is that referring workers so rarely objected to committee decisions on behalf of their clients; the most striking illustration of this passive acquiescence involved several cases of horizontal escalation, in which referring workers requested placement in a group home but accepted psychiatric hospitalization without objection. Objections or appeals were so rare, in fact, as to be considered "unusual" and "exciting" committee events. This acquiescence raises several questions. Why did referring workers not more actively oppose escalated placements on behalf of their clients? Why did the social service centre and the director of youth protection not exercise their legal authority, so that institutions could not acquire control over the disposition of clients?

REFERRING WORKERS

Referring workers were predisposed for several reasons to accept any, rather than no, placement for their clients: (1) their sense of having failed their client; (2) the investment that a referral entailed; (3) the long waiting list for referrals to the committee; and (4) the high cost of failing to place a client.

Sense of Failure

Any decision to refer a young client for placement in a reception centre was painful. Although such placements can be considered as a failure of the social service centre, as a whole, to deal effectively with clients in the community, referring workers often felt the sense of failure personally. As one referring worker put it after his request was refused by the central committee,

You saw what happened there! They treated me as though I didn't do any-
thing with this kid. They make me feel like a failure. Do they really think I
want this kid to go to an institution? They don't know how much time I
spent with this case. At one point you have to ask if it's fair to neglect other
clients and focus on one child, and in this particular case I am not even sure
that giving all my time and energy to this kid would help. Go and tell them
that. I don't even know why I have to feel so bad about it.

Some reception centre workers attributed the referring workers'
propensity to lose touch with their referred clients to this sense of
failure. One Shawbridge social worker even believed that referring
workers simply wanted to forget about the clients they had had to
refer. A Youth Horizons social worker noted that some referring
workers did not even ask casually how their clients were doing.
Whether or not these feelings of failure were justified, they affected
the lives of their young clients. Clearly, presenting cases to a committee of strangers with impressive titles and authority was difficult,
but it was made even more so for the referring workers, in that they
were already uncomfortable about recommending clients to reception
centres. In other words, their sense of having failed with their clients
muted their internal sense of authority to make objections on behalf
of clients.

Investment of Time and Energy

Workers referring a client to the central committee had to come
prepared if they wanted the committee's support for placement. In
addition to preparing their own psychosocial reports, they had to
see that all the other necessary documents were in order; in some
cases, this meant arranging for the client to see a psychologist to
obtain the required evaluation. Referring workers also had to prepare
the client for placement and termination of relationships. Moreover,
they had to present the case to the area-centre placement committee,
before going on to the central committee. Having invested a great
deal of time and energy in preparing for the client's placement,
referring workers were usually predisposed to accept any, rather than
no, placement.

Waiting List for the Central Committee

Once the case was referred to the central committee, there was a
waiting list – not to mention a waiting period of about six weeks.
That meant an extended period of uncertainty for both the referring
workers and their clients. When the referring workers finally

appeared before the central committee, they not only had invested a good deal of time and energy in preparing the case, but were eager to stop "dangling in the air." Unsuccessful requests obliged the referring workers to make good arguments for returning to the committee; they also had another six weeks' wait until the second discussion. Again, the waiting time, as well as the uncertainty, predisposed the workers to accept any, rather than no, placement.

Costs of Not Having a Client Placed

Failure to place referred clients meant more than simply lost time and extended uncertainty. It meant that referring workers had to spend more time with the referred client, neglecting, meanwhile, other clients with better chances for improvement. In this sense, the central committee's decisions to refuse placement not only disrupted referring workers' plans for individual clients, but also their whole "case management" system (Lang 1981). The costs of failing to place a client could also mean the loss of referring workers' credibility – both in the eyes of their clients (the social worker had failed to deliver the recommended program) and, perhaps more importantly, in the eyes of the central committee. After all, that group had refused the referral as clinically inappropriate.

DIRECTOR OF YOUTH PROTECTION

The centralized structure provided the director of youth protection for the anglophone social service centre with a device for handling the internal conflicts that arose following passage of the Youth Protection Act (1977).[8] Because the act imposed new constraints – including specific time limits for dealing with cases, required periodic reports, and the creation of a computerized information system – on the social workers from social service centres and on their work with young clients, the social workers resisted. They viewed the new departments of youth protection as a vehicle for administrative control over their work with clients. In the Ville Marie Social Services Centre, this conflict was amplified by the centre's subdivision into three area-centres, each with a separate administrative head. In effect, the legal authority held by the director of youth protection over the area-centre workers was undermined by his lack of direct organizational authority to review and control their work. He found it difficult to control the resisting social workers.

In this context, the centralized joint-admissions committee had certain advantages. While centralization permitted institutions to control the placement of clients, it also allowed the director of youth protection to monitor and control the work of his own delegates. He did so through outsiders, however, rather than his own department, thus obviating resistance and conflict.

CENTRALIZED CONTROL
OVER ADMISSIONS
AND SOCIAL WORKERS

The provincial Act Respecting Health and Social Services (1971) and the Youth Protection Act (1977) formalized the relations between youth-processing agencies and institutions, but left the shaping of interorganizational admissions committees to the organizations involved. Our analysis shows how, within the anglophone youth-protection network, the interests of both the social service centre's director of youth protection and the reception centres worked to support a centralized committee, thus affecting the disposition of delinquent, neglected, and emotionally disturbed youth.

The centralized committee allowed institutions to control the disposition and institutional placement of adolescent clients through the majority held by the institutional representatives on the committee, the control they held over scarce resources, and their willingness to respect each other's claims to particular clients. The reception centre representatives and psychiatrists were satisfied with the centralized committee: it provided them with routine access to the whole "client market," and allowed them to select "good" clients by mounting a concerted attack on the initial recommendations and clinical judgment of referring workers, thus redefining client problems to suit the resources available.

The social service centre's director of youth protection was also satisfied with the centralized structure because it solved the problems he faced within his own organization. In effect, the centralized committee "supervised" the work of his delegates in ways that he could not.

The referring workers, however, were distinctly dissatisfied with the operation of the centralized committee. Significantly, their anger was not directed at the redefinition of their clients as such. As "good bureaucrats" (Pruger 1973), they understood that client problems need redefinition to fit existing solutions. Indeed, they themselves selected "good clients," redefining these clients' problems for practical purposes (for example, to fit readily available resources, or to avoid resources with long waiting lists); their goal was to balance their client loads and to rid themselves of clients requiring excessive time and energy. Their complaints, therefore, did not concern the redefinition of client problems as such, but rather the way in which this redefinition was done. They objected to the degrading of their professional competence and the violation of their professional right to define and redefine their clients' needs. In fact, referring workers described their appearances before the committee as humiliating "inquisitions" and "cross-examinations."

Although these complaints focused openly on bureaucratic interference into legitimate professional practices, they also conveyed unspoken concerns about the loss of benefits associated with the control over problem-and-needs definition, as well as treatment plans. A study of parole officers, for example, demonstrates how workers manipulate records to threaten parolees, to rid themselves of troublesome ones, and to protect themselves and their superiors (McCleary 1977). Prottas (1979) describes, too, how welfare workers distribute information about benefits unequally, in accordance with their own criteria and preferences, even when standardized information-distribution mechanisms are in place. Blau and Scott (1962) argue, as well, that workers will follow and document those very actions that help them score favourably *vis-à-vis* an organization's statistics. Such practices are also common at the organizational level. Scott (1967b), for example, documents how sheltered workshops for the blind in the United States ended up serving the less needy clients, neglecting those unemployable in commercial settings. Similarly, Teele and Levine (1968) found that child-guidance agencies failed to deal with very difficult clients and those with the greatest need for assistance. These kinds of observations have led Lipsky (1980) to argue that, in fact, "street-level bureaucrats" are making today's social policies. That is, leaving many decisions to the discretion of "street-level" professionals, those who formulate policies are actually losing control over the impact of their initiatives.

But although both top- and street-level bureaucrats did affect the outcome of policies, it was management that largely controlled the process in the centralized committee structure. And members of that group, in turn, had their own interest in maintaining this structure. Thus, even in the face of complaints from referring workers, this structure lasted for three years, the reason being that both the social service centre's management and the director of youth protection benefited from centralization. As a result, professionals' rights with regard to the making of critical decisions affecting their clients – rights built into the Youth Protection Act – were jeopardized. The abrogation of these rights provoked professionals. Even more importantly, however, they undermined the ideology built by the Youth Protection Act around the participation of professionals as youth-protection delegates. A committee structure that so obviously sub-ordinated and humiliated these professionals could not last.

Spurred on by the dissatisfaction of the referring workers, the joint-admissions committee was decentralized in January 1981. That meant that client disposition could be handled in ways which, at least visibly, were more consistent with professional ideals. But, as the next chapter will show, this change did not significantly alter the outcome of placement decisions. It simply shifted control over the process, allowing referring workers to benefit from the greater discretion allowed under the new structure.

CHAPTER SEVEN

Decentralized Disposition of Clients

In 1981, Montreal's anglophone joint-admissions committee was decentralized, thereby altering the structure within which decisions were made concerning the institutional placement of youth. Under the old structure, cases were initially reviewed by one of the placement committees within the three area-centres and then transferred to the central committee for deliberation. Under the new structure, the three placement committees acquired greater authority. Each was expanded to include a reception-centre representative, who spoke for the central committee rather than the reception centre.[1] In theory, the central committee retained authority over placement decisions: the central committee chair, having received placement recommendations from the decentralized committees, could convene subcommittee meetings of reception-centre representatives in the event of conflict. One subcommittee was to deal with the disposition of adolescents, the other with preadolescents.

In practice, however, the central committee existed only on paper. The decentralized committee decisions were treated as final. Indeed, reception centres often began to process clients for admission before the decisions had even reached the central committee. In addition, the subcommittee that was to deal with the disposition of adolescents never met. The preadolescent subcommittee, however, did meet a few times. It seemed that the scarcity of preadolescent clients, in contrast to the surplus of adolescent clients, generated organizational competition and the need to resolve interorganizational conflicts. Under the new structure, therefore, placement decisions were determined within the three decentralized committees. This chapter examines the effects of decentralization on those involved, including the clients.

DECENTRALIZED COMMITTEES
AT WORK

The three decentralized committees were organized along similar lines. Each was chaired by the area-centre's coordinator of family and children's programs and included a nurse, a finder of foster homes, senior or experienced workers with various titles, the review analyst assigned to the area centre by the director of youth protection, and the delegated reception-centre representative. Because the committees dealt at times with decisions other than institutional placement, the reception-centre representative only participated when cases involved institutional placement.

Every two weeks the committees met for between three and four hours to review placement requests presented in person by referring workers; four or five referrals were processed at each meeting. Whereas, in principle, clients were allowed to participate in the meetings, in practice, no clients were ever brought in by the referring workers. Also, although referring workers still had to provide supporting documents, the rules were less strictly enforced than under the previous regime. Workers usually, therefore, presented their cases in a more informal atmosphere.

Placement Decisions

Decentralization did not alter the context within which placement decisions were made; that is, scarce resources and their inflexibility still constrained the disposition of clients. Moreover, placement decisions, tailored to fit the available resources, continued to compromise the clients' needs. The decentralized structure did, however, alter the decision-making process in several ways.

One change was that the decentralized committees permitted referring workers to engage in a much more detailed clinical discussion of their clients' problems than was possible previously, and to give their reasons for recommending placement. However, referring workers often expressed their placement recommendations in general terms, expecting the committee to suggest specific placements. The decentralized committees operated, however, with much less information about institutional resources and their availability than had been the case with the centralized committee. For example, in the new setup, area-centre staff, including both the referring workers and the more experienced committee staff, were usually unfamiliar with the range of programs available at reception centres and psychiatric institutions, not to mention the immediate availability (the length of current waiting lists, for example) of these institutional resources.

The necessary information was supposed to come from the reception-centre representatives who, theoretically at least, attended each committee on a rotating basis; in practice, however, they did not rotate. The reality was that these representatives were critical in determining placement decisions that involved their own reception centres, but added little to discussions of alternate placement options. Thus the number of available options that could be proposed to referring workers was limited. Nevertheless, placement decisions continued to compromise the needs of clients – the practices of attachment and escalation continuing, but in a somewhat different form than was the case under the decentralized structure.

Attachment.   Under the new decentralized structure, attachment was practised less visibly. In effect, the principle of attachment – which dictated that reception centers "owned" the clients they acquired – ruled out the provisional placement of clients in a reception centre until transfer to a more appropriate placement became available. The attachment principle had been visible in the centralized committee, because that structure so clearly raised the transfer issue. That is, the centralized committee, which had included representatives from all institutions and therefore made interorganizational transfer agreements possible, was supposed to coordinate the use of these resources on behalf of clients. This meant that the attachment principle, under the centralized setup, had to be stated overtly from time to time in order to forestall any actual consideration of transfer arrangements.

The decentralized committees, however, with but one reception centre representative apiece, did not provide an interorganizational forum. Transfer agreements could therefore not arise, and thus did not have to be forestalled.

Escalation.   The decentralized structure, although limiting the practice of escalating client placements to fit available resources, actually made the practice of escalation quite visible. Whereas the centralized structure had provided representatives from all institutions with an opportunity to recruit escalated clients for their programs, the decentralized structure limited this opportunity, thus limiting escalation. In effect, the one reception-centre representative on each committee usually confined his or her interest in escalated placements to those related to his or her own reception centres. In one case, a reception-centre representative even tried to avert what he considered to be the horizontal escalation of a client to a psychiatric program.

Thus, if representatives wished to acquire escalated placements for their own reception centres, they had to engage in the process of escalation more openly. No longer could they claim clients indirectly, as in the centralized committee, by privately soliciting support from a nearby colleague. Instead, they had to make the claim alone and directly.

The decentralized committees as a whole also engaged in the process of escalation more openly. Fewer attempts were made to shroud the process in clinical terms and, therefore, fewer attacks were made on the clinical competence of referring workers. For example, when a referring worker, trying to refuse the escalated placement of his client to a cottage, argued the clinical merits of a group-home placement, the committee chair responded by saying, "We know all that, but the fact is that there is no room in group homes." Or take the example of the referring worker who, when he expressed doubt that the court would accept an escalated placement in Shawbridge because it seemed too severe for his client, was informed by both the committee chair and the Shawbridge representative that he could get a court order for a reception-centre placement without identifying Shawbridge. Similarly, another referring worker was cautioned not to mention Shawbridge in court, just as a reminder "to play it on the safe side." The change was one of attitude. Whereas before, in the centralized committee, the clinical competence of the referring workers had been attacked in order to escalate placements, in the decentralized committees, these same referring workers were helped to overcome possible obstacles to escalation, especially the risk of "mismanaging" the court.

The decentralized committees did not mask their practical considerations in clinical rhetoric; nor did they necessarily justify escalated placements through the clinical redefinition of client problems. Even so, clinical grounds were sometimes used to justify escalated placements. For example, one client's escalated placement to a cottage rather than a group home, was justified by the argument that during the wait for a group home to become available the client "would probably become a cottage kid anyway." In another variant of clinical forecasting, the escalated placement of a client at Shawbridge was justified by the client's "pre-delinquent patterns of behaviour."[2] Committee members were really justifying escalated placements in terms of clinical anticipation; they were simply, or so they claimed, doing now what would have to be done in six months anyway. Nevertheless, in the more cooperative and openly practical atmosphere of the decentralized committees, these clinical justifications were less necessary.

IMPACT OF
DECENTRALIZATION

Decentralization did not alter the situation of clients, whose needs continued to be redefined to suit the available resources. Decentralization did, however, substantially affect the interests of other participants in the client-disposition process: the representatives of reception centres and psychiatric institutions, the director of youth protection, and the referring social workers.

Referring Workers

The decentralized committees were more easily accessible to referring workers than the centralized committee had been. However, given these committees' authority regarding such important issues as the removal of adolescents from their natural families, the work of referring workers was critically affected by committee decisions. Nonetheless, the decentralized structure benefited referring workers by reducing the costs of having their requests turned down; other strategic uses of the placement committee process were thus facilitated.

Less awkward committee refusals.   When presenting their cases to the decentralized committees, the referring workers still had to confront challenging questions concerning their placement requests from committe members who wanted to be certain that all other options had been tried. If in doubt about placement in a reception centre, the committee did not hesitate to turn down their requests. But referring workers seemed to accept these refusals more easily from the decentralized committees than they had from the centralized committee. One referring worker explained,

Look, nothing really happened. I thought this kid should be in a reception centre and I got a different opinion on what to do with him ... At least I know where I stand ... Now, if it doesn't work out the way they think, I can always come back and present the case again ... It's our committee, it's here, and we don't have to wait six weeks and then run downtown to hear that we have to wait another few weeks or months until they admit the kid ... If I really have a burning problem I can come in with a day's notice ... I will see what happens and as I said the doors are always open.

In effect, referring workers had less to lose from the decentralized committees' refusals than had been the case under the centralized structure. Not only did these new committees make less exacting demands than the centralized committee regarding the preparation of cases for presentation, but the waiting lists for case presentations were short or non-existent. In some cases, referring workers could even return to the decentralized committees with new information within two weeks. This informality reduced the costs both of making placement requests and of having them turned down. As one referring worker put it, "You can test the water with your toes ... you don't have to dive in to find out that the water is cold."

Strategic use of decentralized committees.   The reduced costs of making placement requests in the decentralized committees allowed referring workers to use these committees in several strategic ways. First, they could more easily "test the market." For instance, committee reactions to placement requests provided workers with useful information about the "marketable" features of clients, about those client attributes that might warrant or rule out placement. Although referring workers did not make placement requests solely to test the market, the information they acquired in so doing was useful in shaping their selection and presentation of clients. The decentralized committees, by reducing the costs of requests, permitted referring workers to realize these benefits more easily and more often.

Second, referring workers could use their easier access to the decentralized committees to "cover" themselves in the event of something going wrong with their clients. By making referrals regularly to the committee, the workers could also avoid the question, "Why didn't you come to us before?" in the event of trouble. As well, referrals to the committee covered workers by involving committee members in the plans for dealing with clients' problems.

Third, the referring workers acquired placement decisions from the decentralized committees as a fail-safe plan. Such a strategy involved asking that clients be placed in a reception centre but, at the same time, continuing to search for other arrangements to keep these clients in the community. A gamble, this strategy clearly lent urgency to the search. As one worker remarked: "After you get a placement decision it's like fighting against the clock ... If you find something in the community before the reception centre wants the client in, you win ... Once he is in, you can't just come and say I want him back ... If you do that, they will start asking you why this kid was referred to them in the first place ... Besides, they are not going to give him up just like that." Not surprisingly, this particular strategy was especially disturbing to the reception centres; indeed, the failure of social workers to "deliver" the clients for whom the decentralized committees had approved placement left the centres with empty beds. This discontent eventually led to a recentralization of the placement process.[3]

Reception Centres and Psychiatric Institutions

Decentralization deprived the reception centres and psychiatric institutions of the control over the disposition of clients that they had enjoyed with the centralized committee. In the decentralized committees, the reception-centre representatives were outnumbered. With only partial access to the "client market," their power was limited, as were their options to select "good clients."

Whereas the decentralized structure limited the access of reception centres to the total client pool, it halted altogether the institutional psychiatric programs' easy access to clients. Psychiatrists, who had represented their institutions "informally" on the centralized committee, were no longer members of the decentralized committees. In the centralized committee set-up, the antipsychiatric views of social workers had been tempered by the four institution-psychiatrist members. In the decentralized committees, however, with the lack of psychiatric institution representatives, antipsychiatric views could emerge. Indeed, the prevalent and critical attitudes toward psychiatric programs were reflected in such statements as: "They are looking for clients in order to boost their budgets"; "They will take anybody who gets close to their criteria"; or "If they don't fill their beds, they will be closed down."

Of course, some psychiatric programs *were* in trouble due to lack of referrals. In an attempt to help, the chair of the largely inactive central committee did, at one point, approach a decentralized committee to promote the most troubled of these programs. But the committee criticized the program's attempt to recruit "motivated clients with a relatively high level of functioning." The committee members felt that the psychiatric programs should be addressing the real problems of psychotic children who were not so cooperative. In view of the antipsychiatric feelings of social workers, psychiatric hospitals tried harder to market their services, but with little success. One particular hospital organized a meeting with the senior workers of key organizations, including the chairpersons of the decentralized committees, to explain and promote their children's services; wine and cheese concluded this unprecedented meeting. Approaches to individual social workers were also attempted. Yet although the psychiatric hospitals tried, they failed to offset the disadvantages of their exclusion from the youth-protection network and its client pool.

Director of Youth Protection

The social service centre's director of youth protection also suffered from decentralization. Not only did he have less influence on placement decisions as a result, but the participation of a review analyst from his department, on each of the decentralized committees, meant a less effective method for controlling area-centre workers than had been the case under the centralized committee set-up. The director of youth protection also lost control over the transfer of clients from the social service to the reception centres under the decentralized structure; that, too, was now largely handled by the chairpersons of the area-centre committees.

These issues of control became particularly pointed when reception-centre complaints began to filter in concerning the failure of area-centre workers to "deliver" the clients that the decentralized committee had agreed to place. Neither the management of the social service centre, nor the director of youth protection, defended their social workers' rights to change clients' treatment plans in light of changing realities and opportunities. No one pointed out, for example, that the prevention of institutionalization should be praised, at least when pursued by the social service centre's social workers. Instead, the social service centre sided with the reception centres. In a meeting at which these complaints were made, a representative from the Ville Marie Social Services Centre's department of youth protection expressed interest in the names of the workers involved. Still another Ville Marie representative commented that the referring workers had complained about the power of the centralized committee but were now abusing the decision-making power given to the area centres.

Thus, whereas the Youth Protection Act emphasized finding solutions for troubled clients that were as close to normal family life as possible, the managers who implemented this act were more concerned about ensuring that social workers did not change their plans to institutionalize clients when new alternatives became available.

RECENTRALIZATION

Contractual agreements between the social service centre and each of the reception centres were dealt with, on a monthly basis, in parity committees. At a parity committee meeting in August 1981, the reception-centre executive in question demanded a return to the centralized structure. He said that although the social service centre operations were none of his business, he could not allow the situation to continue if it threatened his organization. His central complaint was that he was being left with empty beds because social workers were changing their minds after placement decisions had been made. He felt that this did not look good when the network, as a whole, was asking the government for additional institutional beds.

The matter was taken up by the advisory committee, the anglophone network's central-planning body. After a brief deliberation, the committee recentralized the joint-admissions committees, ending one year of decentralization. It seemed that although decentralization had permitted social workers to play the "good bureaucrat" (Pruger 1973), it had undermined the need of their own managers, as well as the managers of reception centres, to play the same game. Indeed, being a "good bureaucrat" in one organization does not always coincide with another organization's goals and needs. As "good bureaucrats" in the social service centre, social workers could portray their clients as appropriate candidates for placement, getting their names placed on reception-centre waiting lists, while continuing to seek other community options involving a different client portrait. For their part, as "good bureaucrats" in the reception centre, reception-centre representatives could not only recruit clients who did not fit their admissions criteria, but could also recruit more clients than the reception centre was able to handle. Although these two counterparts of a "good bureaucrat" could coexist, this was only possible under a centralized disposition of clients. Under the decentralized structure, the social workers' activities were tolerable at those times of the year when the reception centres had more clients than beds, but intolerable during those periods (notably, summers)[4] when the situation was one of more beds than clients.

THE RECENTRALIZED STRUCTURE

Recentralization was implemented in January 1982. By this time, the reception centres had already pulled their representatives out of the decentralized committees. The recentralized structure resembled the original structure, but with a few differences. Most notably, referring workers no longer had to present their cases personally before the central committee.

With recentralization, the reception centres once again had access to the whole client pool. The director of youth protection's control over the decisions of social workers was also restored. Moreover, this control could now be exercised less directly, because the workers no longer presented their referral requests in person.[5] Decisions about clients were now made solely on the basis of written reports from referring workers; their direct reactions to alternative placements were no longer part of the decision-making process. Nor did the referring workers any longer have direct contact with those who made placement decisions for their clients. Thus they were saved from the intolerable confrontations required under the original centralized set-up. For clients, recentralization meant that important decisions about their lives were now being based entirely on written information. When the plans they had agreed upon with their social workers were altered to fit available resources or organizational interests, the clinical judgments of their social workers were not directly challenged. Thus, the new centralized structure satisfied all of the parties involved – except, of course, the clients – by removing opportunities for overt conflict.

By breaking their transactions over clients into two parts, each under separate control, the recentralized admissions committee was able to satisfy the referring workers and reception centres alike. In the first part of the transaction, referring workers were allowed to define, or redefine, their clients' problems in whatever way they thought would facilitate placement. In the second part of the transaction, reception-centre representatives were allowed to review the entire client pool and to redefine client problems to fit the resources available. Although referring workers and reception-centre representatives thus engaged independently in the redefinition of the clients they transferred, the results were the same as they had been in the original centralized committee. The important difference was that referring workers were no longer confronted by a committee that degraded them; no longer could it be said that they had not defined their clients' problems accurately in the first place.

CONCLUSION

Between 1978 and 1982, the anglophone youth-protection network experimented with three structures for handling the disposition and institutional placement of adolescent youths. Several lessons emerged from this experimentation.

From the original centralized structure, network participants learned several important lessons. First, they found that the transfer of clients from the social service centre to reception centres (from social workers to institutions) should be structured in ways that not only did not compromise the professional status of referring workers but also did not directly challenge their mandated role in the placement process. Network participants also learned, this time from the decentralized structure, that client transfers should not be left entirely to low-level professionals, but should be coordinated by the managers of both the social service and the reception centres to ensure that the needs of both organizations are served in the transfer process. The recentralized structure thus solved the problems generated by both the centralized and decentralized structures. With recentralization, the reception centres could assume that their efforts to meet the demand for institutional resources from the social service centre would be matched by the social service centre's parallel efforts to deliver clients when the reception centres needed to fill beds. Furthermore, these interorganizational accommodations could be arranged without humiliating referring workers, for the recentralized structure permitted them to provide the initial definition of their clients' problems, while leaving the final definition to their managers and the reception centre representatives.

The redefinition of client needs to fit available resources must also be understood, however, in the context of general resource allocation. Indeed, the politics of structuring interorganizational relations involve not only a balancing of the participants' benefits, but also a maintenance of the existing system of allocating resources. This latter system is affected by the scarcity of resources, as well as the need to maximize the use of resources. These three interdependent factors affect the interorganizational processing of clients. One of the executives' worst fears, for example, is that resources under their control will be underutilized for excessive time periods. They know that when resources are scarce, funding bodies are more than eager to retrieve unused funds from allocated budgets. They know, too, that in a period of cutbacks it is easier to justify the continuation of existing programs than to request new ones. More importantly, administrators have learned that it is easier to redefine clients than it is to convert and redefine securely funded programs. Although these considerations provide the backdrop against which clients are redefined to fit available resources, this redefinition process requires structures that allow for smooth transactions. This chapter described the evolution of one such structure.

CHAPTER EIGHT

Rights of
Institutionalized Youth

The Youth Protection Act (1977), designed to help problem youth while protecting their rights, includes several devices intended to protect clients from unbridled decision-making about their lives. First, strong checks and balances were created, both between and within the organizations that process young clients; even though, as already observed, within one network at least, the authority given to the social service centre and its director of youth protection never really did "check" the control that reception centres exercised over the disposition of clients.

Second, wide responsibilities and authority were allocated to directors of youth protection to allow them to monitor and review the decisions made about clients through their delegates. Indeed, the complexity of this delegatory arrangement within one social service centre has already been described in the preceding chapters. The upshot is that once the decision has been made to institutionalize a client, directors of youth protection can continue to monitor and review the placement through their delegates.

Third, under the Youth Protection Act, clients for whom "voluntary measures" cannot be arranged are sent to the Youth Court. Those clients for whom "compulsory measures" were envisioned are thus provided with more formal protection of their rights.

Fourth, under the act additional provision was made for the review of decisions about clients: a Youth Protection Committee was established as a system "watchdog".

This chapter examines how these measures failed to protect the rights of clients placed in reception centres in Montreal's anglophone youth-protection network. It focuses, in particular, on the reception centres' methods of managing delegatory arrangements to water down the external review process, thereby acquiring unrestricted, autonomous control over decisions regarding their clients.[1]

THE YOUTH PROTECTION COMMITTEE

The provincial Youth Protection Committee, like the Youth Court, reviewed only compulsory placements; placements made as a "voluntary measure" reached neither the court nor the Youth Protection Committee. Although the Youth Protection Committee was notified of compulsory placements, and could appoint someone to meet with clients who had been in care for at least three months (Quebec 1977, section 63), this option was rarely used. In fact, the recommendation of a group of young people[2] that the Youth Protection Committee use this option to monitor reception centres and detention centres more closely was rejected, on the grounds that the committee had not been provided with sufficient resources, nor a sufficiently clear mandate, to do so. Thus, in terms of resources, information, and mandate, the Youth Protection Committee was not well placed to review the treatment of institutionalized clients on a systematic basis.

THE YOUTH COURT

The Youth Court's authority over compulsory placements was clearer than that of the Youth Protection Committee: it was authorized to approve all compulsory placements. Nevertheless, its ability to review these placements closely was hampered in several ways. First, the directors of youth protection held the authority to select the specific reception centre where the client would be placed; this authority was underlined by a Court of Appeal decision in 1982. Second, as already observed, the social workers who acted as youth-protection delegates learned to avoid mentioning the selected reception centre in court, so as not to jeopardize court support for particular institutional placements. Third, the large size of reception centres, and the variety of institutional programs offered thereby, meant that clients could be internally transferred, even from open to closed units, without having to seek court approval. Clearly, the Youth Court was not equipped to review compulsory placements effectively.

THE DIRECTOR OF YOUTH PROTECTION AND DELEGATES

The limited authority of the Youth Court and the Youth Protection Committee left directors of youth protection, and their delegates, as the only organizational actors with sufficient authority and infor-mation to review and alter, when necessary, the residential treatment plans made by reception centres for their clients. Once clients were placed in reception centres, the Youth Protection Act required direc-tors of youth protection to monitor and review their placement on a periodic basis "to determine if the child's situation warrants addi-tional measures or measures different from those being applied" (Quebec 1977, section 57).

The review process is carried out after the director of youth pro-tection has formally delegated authority to delegates. For each client the director assigns authority, via a written contract, to a delegate who then "holds the delegation." Periodic reports from delegates provide the director of youth protection with information about all clients placed in reception centres. Within the anglophone network, four alternative delegation arrangements have been instituted. The first entails using a social worker from the social service centre (the referring worker), to act as the delegate when the client is in the community; that social worker will continue to hold the delegation responsibility and to follow the client in the reception centre. The second arrangement involves a transfer of the delegation to a social worker at the social service centre, who specializes in institutional care. The third involves a transfer of the delegation to a social worker at the reception centre (a practice referred to as "full delegation"). The fourth entails a sharing of the delegation between social workers at both the social service and reception centres (a practice referred to as "partial" or "double" delegation).

In theory, the authority to protect clients and their rights assigned to the director of youth protection threatened the autonomy of recep-tion centres, as well as the legitimacy of the latter's methods of dealing with clients. In practice, however, the reception centres in the net-work studied were able to manage these provisions for "external review" in ways that enhanced their public image and, at times, even led to increased autonomy in determining treatment plans for clients.

DILUTING THE EXTERNAL REVIEW PROCESS

Although their response to the potential threat presented by the director of youth protection and his delegates was different, and although they employed a different delegation option, the two recep-tion centres in the network managed to dilute, or water down, the external review process. Under two different structural arrangements, the external review process was rendered meaningless.

Shawbridge Model

Shawbridge openly objected to external review, arguing that if adolescents were to be entrusted to its care, external authorities should not be allowed to interfere with the institution's treatment methods. Shawbridge dealt with the threat to its autonomy in two ways: it decided that a court order would be required as a condition for client admissions; it also hired its own social workers to act as youth-protection delegates.

The court-order policy.   Shawbridge's court-order policy preserved the institution's right to control admissions. In light of its long war – The Boys' Farm against court-controlled admissions – such a policy might seem surprising. But Shawbridge could now use the new authority of the youth-protection network vis-à-vis the disposition of clients – not only to select clients, but also to control the decisions of the court. As a participant in the joint-admissions committee, Shawbridge could now select clients but have them processed in court as compulsory, unspecified placements recommended by the youth-protection network as a whole. Indeed, Shawbridge's court-order policy protected its control over admissions from the director of youth protection's newly mandated authority to place "voluntary" clients in institutions. In fact, although the director of youth protection regarded Shawbridge's court-order policy as an infringement on his authority, he did not openly contest the policy by assigning clients to Shawbridge without a court-order.[3] Shawbridge's court-order policy thus meant that the institution could control its admissions without interference by the director of youth protection and without risking greater control by the court. Indeed, court-orders implied external review and helped to legitimate placements as just.

Employment of its own social workers.   Shawbridge's even more pointed method of handling the threat to its autonomy posed by the external review process was to employ its own staff of social workers as youth-protection delegates. Thus Shawbridge advocated the third delegatory arrangement described above, that of "full delegation": the transfer, from the referring worker to a reception-centre social worker, of the delegated authority to monitor and review a client's placement. This arrangement, like the court-order policy, infringed on the authority assigned by law to social service centres. The social service centre, however, never openly contested the practice.[4]

Shawbridge argued that "full delegation" provided not only the reception centre with flexibility in clinical decision-making, but also the client with guaranteed continuity of service. Because the anglophone social service centre – which was Shawbridge's primary source of clients – agreed to the full delegation policy, both the director of youth protection and the court based their "external" reviews of clients placed at Shawbridge entirely on material provided by the reception centre's own employees. Moreover, Shawbridge expected these delegates to be loyal to the reception centre rather than to the director of youth protection (DYP); this expectation was clearly stated in a document interpreting the Youth Protection Act:

As a delegate of the DYP, this individual is directly responsible to the DYP and carries the powers and obligations delegated to him or her. As an employee of Shawbridge, however, this person is, first and foremost, bound by the conditions of employment of Shawbridge and by the standards of professional casework practice. In addition, he or she is held accountable by the policies, procedures and supervisory structure of this agency. In view of Shawbridge's primary responsibility for taking charge of the child as the Court/DYP's location of choice, it is therefore understood that the caseworker cannot operate independently of the constraints, obligations and expectations of this agency. (Shawbridge Youth Centre 1980, 30–1)

The Shawbridge representative also emphasized this policy during parity committee meetings with the social service centre, as a way of underlining the delegation to Shawbridge of the director of youth protection's authority. Shawbridge, in turn, delegated individual workers to each client.

The reception centre's management and social workers (delegates) were candid about their belief that Shawbridge should present these external bodies with reports having an internal consensus about both the client's progress and the recommended treatment plans. The social workers pointed out that clients were allowed to read their files and argued that exposure to conflicting views only confuses children. It is worth noting, however, that most clients at Shawbridge are teenagers.

The social workers also regarded their periodic written reports to the director of youth protection as just an administrative ritual, the only feedback being brief comments such as "keep up the good work" and "good report." One worker noted that these comments made him feel as if he, himself, were in a behaviour modification program. Interestingly, the social workers did not experience role conflict regarding the practice of consensus reporting, even when they disagreed with the reports. Nevertheless, and more importantly, the workers strongly believed in the reception centre's right to autonomous control over the treatment of clients. As one of them put it: "If I send a car to the garage I don't tell the mechanics what tools to use. There are some trust relationships ... I expect that if somebody refers a kid to Shawbridge he or she should trust Shawbridge to do the job."

The social workers also favoured consensus reports to the Youth Court. One felt that the court was not equipped to deal with conflicting recommendations; another contended that judges did not want to hear conflicting views, citing an instance in which a judge had asked the disputing parties to reach an agreement before returning to him. Nevertheless, the social workers were disturbed when they had to present recommendations in court that they, themselves, had opposed within the agency. The reception centre's novel solution to this problem was to send the residential program coordinators to court, thus allocating responsibility for the official presentation of treatment plans and any changes – some of which were internally disputed by social workers – to the originators of the plans. Whereas this policy reduced the intensity of role conflicts, another policy change, under which Shawbridge stopped asking the court to authorize the internal transfer of clients from one program to another, actually reduced the need to go to court. This policy shift meant that the interests of the professional staff superseded the view of the reception centre's legal adviser, who held that "a child has a right to be heard in court, especially when the outcome of an internal transfer is a further restriction of freedom."

The importance of consensus reports, and of the nonparticipation of courts in decision-making regarding internal transfers, was demonstrated by occasional public conflicts between reception-centre and social-service-centre delegates. But such conflicts arose only sporadically, when clients were referred from the two, small, social service centres[5] that practised "double delegation" (the fourth delegatory option); that is, when the delegation was shared between social workers from the social service and reception centres. In these "double delegation" situations, the views of the social-service-centre delegate responsible for the overall welfare of the child carried great weight with the Youth Court; in fact, the reception centre usually lost all conflicts with this delegate over treatment plans for the client. To avoid such situations, the delegates were invited to case conferences preceding legal action. If the attempts at co-optation were unsuccessful, Shawbridge sometimes yielded to the delegate's views, rather than proceed to confrontation and probable defeat in court.

Under the Shawbridge model, court reviews were ceremonial: the appearance of a just and external review was simply reinforced by documentation that revealed nothing but consensus and harmony among the various professionals involved. Nonetheless, Shawbridge acquired legitimacy from the appearance of legal justice, inasmuch as court procedures are widely understood to represent the ideal model of due process and justice.

Shawbridge was able, then, to manage the threats to its autonomy posed by the provisions for external review by directly controlling its youth-protection delegates as employees and by using the ceremonial appearance of legal justice.

Youth Horizons Model

Youth Horizons dealt with threats to its autonomy in a completely different way. Because most of its clients were placed under the "voluntary measures" provision of the Youth Protection Act, the court presentations of the youth-protection delegates did not constitute central ceremonial activities. Nor did Youth Horizons employ its own social workers, contracting them instead from the social service centre[6] (the second delegatory option described above). In fact, when clients were placed at Youth Horizons, the delegation of authority to monitor and review their placements was transferred – from the referring worker to another social worker from the social service centre, a specialist in institutional care.

The social workers who acted as youth-protection delegates for clients at Youth Horizons were therefore not constrained by demands for loyalty to the reception centre, backed by an implicit threat to their jobs. Nevertheless, they faced constraints originating from the dynamics of their Youth Horizon treatment teams. Delegates, once assigned to one or two treatment teams, worked closely within their teams. They had to deal with conflicts arising from their difficulties in reconciling teamwork with their commitment to their Youth Protection duties, or else request another assignment within the social service centre.

The management of the social service centre was well aware of the risks of co-optation associated with youth-protection delegates coming under the continuing influence of their reception-centre teammates. A new policy document – one that would have allowed workers to rotate among teams[7] – was drawn up, listing certain benefits that the current policy, by implication, did not have. For instance, the new policy would

- create psychological "distance" between the social worker and cottage life;
- provide possibilities for the "treatment-matching" of social worker and client;

- enable the social worker to focus on families rather than cottages;
- restore the social worker to the role of monitoring the global treatment plan while remaining peripheral to clients in residence;
- provide a better link with the social service centre's home-base.

The new policy was not implemented however, leaving delegates open to co-optation by the Youth Horizons' treatment teams. The ways they were co-opted and the "accounts" (Scott and Lyman 1968) they used to justify their behaviour as loyal team members are described elsewhere (Teram 1986). For the purposes of this analysis, it is sufficient to observe that co-optation made their external reviews of institutional placements just as ceremonial as those at Shawbridge.

Obviously, the Shawbridge delegates participated ceremonially in the external review process because they were employed by the reception centre, whose activities they were presumably intended to monitor and review. The motives of the delegates at Youth Horizons were more complex, however, more closely related to the dynamics of teamwork: the diffusion of role differences; the desire to belong to a group; the daily interdependencies and trade-offs among team members; and, in this context, the costs of resorting to formal authority and external support during conflicts with team members.

Conflicts between delegates and members of Youth Horizons' staff and management arose around the same kinds of issues that produced internal disputes at Shawbridge: treatment plans for clients; alterations in these plans; and the internal transfer of clients from one program to another. The accepted method of dealing with such conflicts was to call for a case conference with Youth Horizons' managerial staff, on the one hand, and the social work supervisors from the social service centre, on the other. The director of youth protection was not involved in these meetings; furthermore, the conflicts over clients addressed and resolved during these meetings were never reflected in the periodic reports he received. Again, consensus reports were the norm. Thus, the director of youth protection was not in a position to check the authority of Youth Horizons over its clients, as had been envisioned in the Youth Protection Act.

The delegates themselves also avoided making explicit use of their delegated youth-protection authority to affect reception-centre decisions on behalf of their clients. When delegates did use their authority, it was in conjunction with reception-centre staff, and mostly in dealings with uncooperative clients. By failing to use their delegated authority on behalf of institutionalized clients, the social workers, by their own admission, tolerated practices at Youth Horizons that would never have been tolerated in families. Indeed, if they had seen such practices in family settings, they would have exercised their Youth Protection authority on behalf of the clients. Moreover, the delegates carefully used vague terms, such as "excessive use of authority," "inconsistent or unrealistic treatment plans," and "procrastination," when criticizing these institutional practices toward their clients.

Although the director of youth protection believed that workers knew they would come to him with any problem, his delegates for the clients at Youth Horizons claimed that they received an indirect message of disinterest regarding conflicts with the reception centre over client treatment. And their supervisors delivered the same message, albeit more clearly and directly.[8] For example, one stated:

Youth Horizons is like a child and it is in its early development and if the Director of Youth Protection comes and makes comments about every small thing it is not going to help ... the director of youth protection's involvement in Youth Horizons' affairs can only add confusion. The direction has to be made clear and like every child, Youth Horizons makes mistakes and falls on its bum and then gets up and starts walking and tumbles again ... But you have to let them (Youth Horizons) go through the process without interference ... director of youth protection intervention is not going to help. They have enough motivation here to change and to improve and you have to give them the opportunity to form their identity.

THE COST OF AVOIDING CONFLICT

The co-optation of youth-protection delegates as well as the practice of consensus-reporting at both Shawbridge and Youth Horizons indicate that the crucial legislated mechanisms for protecting the interests and rights of institutionalized youth – external review by the Youth Court and by the director of youth protection – were sacrificed for the sake of "organizational peace."

Perhaps the Youth Protection Act relied too heavily on the workers' willingness to remain within the boundaries of their organizations and roles. This present analysis demonstrates that social workers, when faced with conflicting expectations (role conflicts) will, in fact, cross organizational boundaries (as at Youth Horizons) or role boundaries (as at Shawbridge), thereby defeating the purposes for which these boundaries were established. But in crossing these boundaries, workers are co-opted: "By passing the boundary and becoming a functioning member of the (new) organization, the person takes on some of the coding system of the organization since he accepts some of its norms and values, absorbs some of its subculture and develops shared expectations and values with other members" (Katz and Kahn 1966, 228).

Workers, such as the youth protection delegates, who occupy "boundary-spanning roles" – roles that entail interaction with other organizations – experience more role conflict than those workers positioned deep within an organization (Kahn et al 1964). This is understandable, given the constant exposure of "boundary spanners" to expectations originating with the workers, managers, and clients (role senders) of more than one organization. Although, in this study, the director of youth protection was technically an internal role sender for Youth Horizons' delegates and an external one for Shaw-bridge delegates, this difference affected only slightly the delegates' abilities to protect either the rights and interests of youth, or the degree of the intersender's role conflicts. At Shawbridge, the social workers' potential role conflicts were somewhat reduced by their perception that the director of youth protection expected little from them other than high-quality on-time reports. The Shawbridge del-egates also faced fewer potential role conflicts because of their employment at a reception centre rather than a social service centre; doubts were reduced as to where their loyalty should lie, and the potential sanctions for disloyalty were clear. Even when these dele-gates had doubts about the legitimacy of consensus reporting or about presenting recommendations in court that they themselves opposed, these potential sanctions helped to deter dissent and resolve conflict.[9]

It is, nevertheless, significant that Shawbridge social workers rarely referred to such sanctions when explaining their actions, instead providing other justifications for the practices that made them uncomfortable.[10] Some of these justifications have already been men-tioned: "It's better for the child not to read conflicting reports"; "Reports of conflicts can only disturb the administration of the recep-tion center"; or "Shawbridge has its own system of checks and bal-ances and knows what it is doing." To these, it is important to add the more formal arguments: "We do not make decisions, we only make recommendations to the court. In court we represent Shaw-bridge, the child's lawyer represents the child and we try to make sure that the child will have a lawyer." Even when their actions were inconsistent with their legislated role as youth protection delegates, Shawbridge social workers could nevertheless define their actions and resolve the potential role conflicts in what were, to them, pro-fessionally acceptable terms.

At Youth Horizons, the team model controlled the work of boundary spanners and resolved the potential role conflicts rather differently. In effect, the ultimate sanction of hiring and firing delegates was unavailable at Youth Horizons; thus the subordination of delegates to teamwork adjustment processes played a crucial role in controlling the delegates' use of their youth protection authority. For example, the Youth Horizons' delegates did not use formal arguments, as did the Shawbridge delegates, to explain and justify their actions. Even the sanctions they faced for disloyalty to reception centre teammates were informal: the cold shoulder; no smile or "good morning;" and, more importantly, no reciprocal accommodations and adjustments when the need arose. The Youth Horizons' delegates who solved their problems within their teams not only avoided bitter feelings on the part of teammates, but also advanced themselves as loyal team members who played according to accepted rules, thereby earning the right to reciprocal accommodations and adjustments when needed. At Youth Horizons, therefore, the maintenance of good working relations within teams helped delegates to reduce potential role conflicts as boundary spanners.

The unclear messages that delegates at both reception centres received from the director of youth protection contributed to their reliance upon internal mutual adjustments, rather than external authority, in making plans for clients. Whether these mutual adjustments were intraorganizational (as at Shawbridge) or interorganizational (as at Youth Horizons) was irrelevant. At both reception centres, delegates chose to "live and let live," to rely on persuasion rather than formal authority when advancing their views, and to cooperate with others in order to get their own work done. At both reception centres, delegates regarded it as unwise to write reports to the director of youth protection criticizing the reception centre's treatment of clients. Rather they resolved conflicts through internally legitimate processes that, although they might take longer, did not harm the good working relations that might take even longer to rebuild.

CHAPTER NINE

Conclusion

This case study has examined how, at different points in the history of a large, Canadian, youth-in-trouble network, public policies affecting the disposition of problem youth have shaped, and been shaped by, youth-processing organizations. The study has focused on the politics of client recruitment – the strategies used by youth-processing organizations to control the selection of clients. The early historical material demonstrates the link between these strategies and organizational interests; the more current material highlights the emergent role of professionals in youth-processing organizations as an effective method for obscuring and legitimating these interests.

TRANSFORMATION OF CLIENT-RECRUITMENT STRATEGIES

The increased involvement of professional social workers, psychologists, and psychiatrists in the disposition of delinquent, neglected, and emotionally disturbed youth had a profound impact on the client-recruitment strategies of youth-processing organizations. Indeed, the involvement of professionals altered, masked, and legitimated organizational strategies built on individualized assessment and the case-by-case selection of clients. The effectiveness of these subtle and inconspicuous strategies can be clearly seen against the backdrop of earlier, balder and less successful strategies.

The early efforts of The Boys' Farm to acquire control over the size and composition of its client population were intended to expand its population but maintain its orientation toward the reform of "normal bad boys" – its traditional target population. Its strategies for increasing the supply of reformable youth at that time were direct:

advertising addressed to parents experiencing difficulties with their children, and political lobbying for indefinite, as well as longer, sentences. These client-recruitment strategies were also broad, in the sense that they only occasionally focused on individual clients as such. Although the unfitness of particular boys for discharge was occasionally used as an argument to extend their sentences, The Boys' Farm usually favoured broad strategies (the indefinite sentence, sentences of not less than two years, and court consultations regarding the actual release date of sentenced clients) as a way of solving its population crises. Similarly broad strategies were also adopted to control the admission of older boys. Moreover, although confrontations between the institution and the juvenile court focused at times on individual cases, the confrontation in those early years focused more on the broader and more generic issues of age, as well as on the opening of locked units.

These early client-recruitment strategies were not masked as concern for the "best interests" of delinquent youth. Indeed, the board's reluctance to accommodate older boys, in spite of appeals from the court and its own staff, actually increased the number of boys sent to adult prisons. Some institutional staff members expressed open discomfort about their participation in this process. They were unable, however, to alter board policy in ways that would take the best interests of youth into account; for example, through institutional adjustments to accommodate new client populations and needs.

In 1960, the nature of the strategies began to shift – away from these generic client-recruitment strategies, to strategies that focused on the specific characteristics of individual clients. For example, in an attempt to control the admission of emotionally disturbed clients, The Boys' Farm introduced a three-month trial period; clients that did not "respond to treatment" – the assessments were made by visiting psychiatrists – could then be rejected. This was the first client-admission strategy to emphasize the suitability of individual clients for institutional services. Indeed, the notion of individual assessment was introduced at this time into the conflict between all of Montreal's youth-protection schools and the court, the goal being to screen out emotionally disturbed clients and send "inadmissible cases" back to court.

The concept of individual assessment was to become the building block for later client-recruitment strategies, strategies less visible than the earlier generic ones. Although introduced as a policy for distinguishing between clients who could benefit from the institution and those who could not, individual assessment made less visible those organizational efforts to control admissions for other reasons. Indeed, the institution's long and continuing interest in controlling the selection of clients was now hidden in decisions to admit or refuse clients on a case-by-case basis.

The introduction of individualized assessment as a client-recruitment strategy, although contested by the court, was nonetheless the first step towards the "differential treatment" ideology that eventually legitimated institutional control over admissions. The court continued to resist the institution's selective admissions policy due to its own emphasis on the legal and jurisdictional aspects of client processing. However, the concept of selective admissions was consistent with the orientations of social service agencies and professionals. When the disposition of problem youth was transferred to social service professionals, reception centres such as Shawbridge found themselves in a comfortable environment – one that emphasized professional self-regulation and autonomy. This was a natural environment for the ideology, language, and techniques that reduced the visibility of organizational interests previously exposed in arguments and direct confrontations with the court.

Thus, although a selective admissions policy based on individual assessment may serve the best interests of clients, it is also singularly well equipped – through its legitimacy and invisibility – to serve the best interests of organizations.

CONSTRUCTION AND DEFENCE OF PROFESSIONAL IMAGE

The professionalization of youth-processing organizations built legitimacy not only by sponsoring technologies that concealed links between organizational interests and client recruitment, but also by providing themselves with a "perfect theory" for presenting legitimating myths about themselves. As Meyer and Scott (1983, 201) observe: "A completely legitimate organization would be one about which no question could be raised. Every goal is specified, unquestionable, and reasonably important. Every technical means is adequate and has no alternative. Every human and external resource used is necessary and adequate. Every aspect of the control system is complete and without alternative ... Perfect legitimation is perfect theory, complete (i.e. without uncertainty) and confronted by no alternatives." In that sense, this book describes the development of a "perfect theory," by a respected institution, in what is considered to be one of the most progressive child-welfare systems in Canada (LeBlanc and Beaumont 1988). In essence, this "perfect theory" claims that the institution has the right to control its admissions and treatment of clients without external interference – because of its professional expertise.

Without first-hand observations of the actual processes through which clients are defined and redefined, all child-welfare systems might well be termed "progressive." The elaborate formal structures and procedures that increasingly characterize these systems only reinforce this impression. In the child-welfare system studied in this book, the three ways of structuring the joint-admissions committee all seemed rational. Theoretically, each provided a solution to the need for coordinating the disposition of clients in a child-welfare network with scarce institutional resources. Organizational theorists could, no doubt, debate the weaknesses and advantages of these three structures endlessly. Indeed, without first-hand observation, the network's experiments with different structures might well look like an admirable search for the "best" structure.

Our observations suggest, however, that this so-called search did not, in fact, benefit the clients. Apparently, a "best structure" meant one thing to institutions and another to agency social workers; there was, moreover, a structure that "best" reconciled the interests of both. In the end, however, these alterations made little difference to the clients; the same practical considerations governed their disposition and escalated their placements. In fact, structures that seem rational because they enhanced interorganizational coordination may actually promote harmony at the expense of clients, by reducing the useful conflicts that might otherwise protect clients' interests and rights (Hawkins and Tiedeman 1975). As well, neither professionals nor youth-processing organizations are likely to favour interorganizational and interprofessional conflicts, because such conflicts will only expose both the indeterminate technologies and the practical considerations involved in disposition decisions. Without such exposure, however, adolescent clients (and their parents) remain mystified by the language of treatment and by their exclusion from the discussions and settings in which important decisions about their lives are being made.

The silencing of clients is particularly significant because the legitimacy of youth-processing organizations has not been acquired through demonstrated evidence as to their actual effectiveness in treating these clients. In fact, the unstated, yet prevailing, assumption that professionalized organizations are effective in treating clients is the result, not the source, of organizational legitimacy. Indeed, the so-called theory that legitimates youth-processing organizations may be termed "perfect" primarily because it has not required such evidence. Moreover, as Fombrun (1986, 418) observes, "to claim effectiveness for surviving organizations is simply to ignore the process of contextualization through which effectiveness is itself defined and rationalized." In a context in which professionals have gained exclusive control over the definition of client problems, treatment plans, and their success, there can be no independent evidence concerning effectiveness of treatment, nor any incentive to review the self-generated evidence.

Professionals nonetheless work in organizations with distinct boundaries and domains. In juvenile delinquency and child-welfare systems, for example, they have been given mandates to perform certain duties, some of which include the examination of what other professionals and organizations do for clients. In this regard, the Youth Protection Act (1977) was particularly explicit in introducing checks and balances into the system. As such, by creating arenas where the premises of professionalism and organizational autonomy could have been challenged, this legislation threatened the ability of youth-processing organizations to project certain myths about themselves and to sustain their "theory."

Youth-processing organizations responded effectively to this threat, however, and managed to construct their relations with one another in ways that enhanced their legitimacy. For example, the centralized joint-admissions committee challenged a fundamental principle among professionals; namely, that professionals who work directly with clients should make the decisions about them. Although decentralization restored this principle, it limited the reception centres' access to the pool of clients and encouraged speculation on the part of referring workers. By eliminating direct confrontation over these issues, recentralization provided a structure for building inter-organizational relations of mutual benefit; it also helped along the process of mutual legitimation.

The Youth Protection Act threatened the professional autonomy and legitimacy of reception centres as well, by introducing legal provisions for external review of, and intervention into, what reception centres considered their "own business." Moreover, although the Youth Protection Act benefited reception centres by limiting the authority of the court over client disposition, it generated a new, and potentially more extensive, formal authority over client disposition and treatment. The director of youth protection for each network was given authority to alter individual treatment plans and thus to interfere with the internal operation of institutions – something that the court in previous years had tried but failed to do. Furthermore, even though institutions had not been formally obligated to yield to court demands regarding their internal operation, similar demands from the director of youth protection were sanctioned by mandated authority; they were also legitimated as responses to the needs of individual clients.

Exercising this authority had the potential to shake the control that institutions had acquired through the deployment of professional concepts such as differential treatment; it could also cast doubt on the legitimacy of the network itself. Clearly, if referrals to reception centers were to appear appropriate and clinically justified, the treatment plans developed by these institutions also had to appear correct and clinically justified. Otherwise, the adequacy of the theory and principles that the network's youth-processing organizations attempted to project would be open to dispute. Furthermore, because both reception centres and social service centres employed professionals – who usually preferred to avoid external scrutiny of their knowledge and technologies – open manifestations of mutual distrust were unwise, undesirable, and unlikely.

In the past, such criticism originating from professional quarters led to a population crisis at The Boys' Farm. Indeed, Dr Marcilio and the juvenile court-assessment clinic had had little to lose by recommending that commitments to that institution be avoided. Nor did the clinic's legitimacy depend on what The Boys' Farm said or thought about the clinic's operation, particularly given the Farm's own lack of professional staff. On these grounds, that institution could have been properly criticized and excluded from the ranks of professionalized organizations. By the time the Youth Protection Act was introduced, however, the Farm had managed to transform its status and capitalize on its professional image.

This image of legitimacy can no longer be projected separately from the image of other organizations in the network; nor can it be challenged independently from the image, and resources, of the network as a whole. For example, the reception centres complained that referring workers' speculative requests for placements left them with empty beds; they emphasized the inappropriateness of this practice at a time when the network as a whole was requesting additional institutional resources. Thus, given the interdependence of the social service and reception centres, the organizational and interorganizational processes had to converge in order to project a "perfect theory." Moreover, legal provisions alien to this legitimizing ideology had to be neutralized through interorganizational and intraorganizational processes, and through structures that reinforce an impression of professionalism and consensus.

The ceremonies performed under the banner of "the protection of children's rights" are critical to the current youth-in-trouble system's continuing legitimacy. The institutionalization of these rights (McDougall 1985) ensures that these legal provisions will remain intact. But these provisions have largely functioned to create the impression of "doing good," rather than to ensure a genuine review of what is being done for young people. Nevertheless, this impression is important for both government and professionals. For government, it buffers external demands for change, improvement, and the spending of more money on alternatives that address the source of adolescent problems. For professionals and the agencies employing them, it substantiates their claim that their privileged position is based on the ownership of exclusive useful knowledge.

The politics of client recruitment have thus come to involve symbiotic relations between the provincial government and the network of organizations it funds. Over the eighty-year period we have described, these relations have become complex. At one time, the government funded, but did not otherwise directly affect, the operation of youth-processing organizations. Now government has become the master of "infrastructure manipulation" (Thompson 1974), while youth-processing organizations have become skillful at using the infrastructure for their own purposes.

REFLECTIONS ON RECENT POLICY DEVELOPMENTS

Both the United States and Canada are once again at a turning point regarding their juvenile delinquency policies. In 1984, Canada's Juvenile Delinquents Act (1908) was replaced by the Young Offenders Act. On the one hand, the new act sponsors a renewed concern for justice in terms of young peoples' accountability regarding violations of the federal criminal code, determinate rather than indeterminate sentences, and the greater protection of legal and procedural rights in the youth court. In this sense, the Young Offenders Act is criminal legislation, cut-and-dried (Rothman and Scattolin 1983, 57). On the other hand, the Young Offenders Act also sponsors "alternative measures" for minor and first offenders as a way of avoiding the youth court. The police or crown prosecutor, for instance, may refer young offenders to community agencies or programs when they are "satisfied that alternative measures would be 'appropriate, having regard to the needs of the young person and the interests of society,' and that sufficient evidence exists to take the case to court" (Bala 1988).

In the United States, the head of the Office of Juvenile Justice and Delinquency Prevention emphasizes the need to hold young offenders accountable for their action (Regnery 1986). Recent reviews of national trends in the United States (Curran 1988; Krisberg et al

1986) argue that all levels of the U.S. delinquency-processing system have been taking a harder line toward juvenile delinquents. Despite declines in the size of the youth population and the number of juvenile arrests, the number of police referrals to court have increased, as has the severity of imposed sanctions. These same reviews also indicate that the downward trend in training-school admissions has reversed itself; evidently the lengths of stay, in both training schools and detention centres, have risen as well.

These policy changes are taking place in Canada and the United States even though the failure of previous reforms is still being debated. The debate has centred on the unintended "net-widening" and "transinstitutionalizing" effects of diversion and deinstitutionalization (see Klein 1979, Moyer 1980, Warren 1981, Lerman 1982, Cohen 1985, Trepanier 1983). In Quebec, this discussion focuses on the consequences of the 1977 Youth Protection Act – an act that was intended to divert neglected and delinquent youths from stigmatizing contacts with the juvenile court by referring them, for initial screening, to social service centres and their directors of youth protection. In 1979, the first year of its operation, this diversion dramatically reduced the number of youths referred by the police for formal processing, as well as the number of youths referred to court following initial screening. From 1980 to 1983, however, there were equally dramatic reversals: the number of police referrals for screening increased; the number of referrals from directors of youth protection to court increased, and court dispositions became more severe (Trepanier 1983, 1986).

The Youth Protection Act increased police referrals by "turning the decision of the police into a nondecision" (Doob 1983). Rather than making the decision to lay charges or let a youth go, the police could turn the decision over to directors of youth protection. Thus, the net was widened to include youths who, formerly, would simply have been released by the police (Trepanier 1983, 1986).

In practice, directors of youth protection did not substitute "voluntary measures" for court referrals. Within Montreal's anglophone network, the most obvious reason for increased court referrals from the director of youth protection was the requirement of a court order as a condition of admission, to one of the network's largest reception centres (Shawbridge), thus inflating the number of anglophone youths sent to court. In this sense, court referrals were partly generated by institutional policy, rather than by the specific misconduct or lack of voluntary cooperation of individual youths.

In anticipation of the new federal Young Offenders Act implemented in 1984, the Province of Quebec established a special parliamentary commission in 1981 to review the operation of its Youth

Protection Act. As the result of recommendations made in the Char-bonneau report (Quebec 1982), the Youth Protection Act was amended in 1984 to return the initial screening of young offenders to the justice system (Rothman and Scattolin 1983; Hackler 1983; LeBlanc and Beaumont 1988). The primary impact of the federal Young Offenders Act in the Province of Quebec has therefore been to shore up the interests, claims, and complaints of the justice pro-fessionals, including police, prosecutors, defense lawyers, juvenile court judges, and probation officers.

What effects will this latest shift of public policy have on youth-processing organizations and the disposition of clients? Hackler (1983) predicts that the transfer of responsibility and workload, from the Province of Quebec's Department of Social Affairs back to the Department of Justice, will expand the power and resources of delin-quency networks at the possible expense of youth-protection net-works. But as Hackler also observes:

Almost all systems in North America have theoretically different streams for protection and delinquency cases, but very often the police come into contact with juveniles who have stolen *and* who live in less than desirable situations. At every step in the system professionals make decisions that balance the protection of society, justice, child welfare and the responsibility of the juvenile; but they also consider the consequences of certain types of deci-sions. The agents of the system continually think ahead, and hence it is not surprising that they "use" the courts, the welfare system, the law, and other resources as tools to achieve desired goals. (Hackler 1983, 359)

From this point of view, the most recent shift of public policy may simply entail extending to justice professionals the same opportu-nities as those offered to child-welfare professionals: to screen clients, to define the nature of client troubles in their own professional terms, and to acquire a degree of control over their disposition. Moreover, clients may circulate in new ways, within and across the delinquency, youth-protection, and psychiatric networks, as their troubles are defined or changed by their experiences within the system.

It is not yet known how youth-processing organizations have dealt with the challenges presented by the Young Offenders Act. To date, most of the material available (for example, Hudson, Hornick, and Burrows 1988) deals with the formal aspects of the legislation and its implementation in different provinces. Our study has demon-strated, however, that formal arrangements can be used by youth-processing organizations in ways that can only be discovered through close observation. Like the Youth Protection Act, the new legislation introduces new participants and will require youth-processing organizations to modify their practices. Taking the history of the network as a guide, we would argue that most of the challenges presented by the latest legislation are once again related to control over admissions and treatment plans.

With its particular emphasis on the delivery of criminal justice in its traditional form, the Young Offenders Act reconstitutes the relevance of legal procedures and definitions. The act seems to restore, at least partially, the kind of court control over the commitment of young offenders that The Boys' Farm struggled for so long to curtail. Although it reintroduces a clear distinction between delinquency and protection cases, it also introduces complexities in terms of the mix of clients placed in reception centres, some of whom will be committed as young offenders by the court, while others will be referred by the director of youth protection (Caputo and Bracken 1988).

Insofar as judges take more explicit charge of the disposition of young offenders, they may also become more active in intervening on behalf of youths who complain about escalated placements made by the director of youth protection. In a recent case involving a sixteen-year-old boy, for example, a youth-court judge "took the unusual step of naming the institution where the boy must be placed,"[1] thereby challenging the right of the directors of youth protection to choose the appropriate placement. He did not accept the director of youth protection's argument that placing the boy in closed custody (rather than open custody, as the director of youth protection had recommended) was justified by the lack of resources. It is significant that, in this context, the revised Youth Protection Act (1984) nevertheless explicitly justifies such compromises, allowing those who make placement decisions to take "into consideration the organization and resources of existing establishments or agencies" (Quebec 1984, chapter 4, 11.1). This case, then, not only demonstrates the costs of speaking openly about the practical reasons governing the disposition of clients, but also provides an informative contrast to the clinical justifications for escalation described in our study. At the same time, it is possible that judges have become more sensitized to escalated youth-protection placements, now that the Young Offenders Act requires them to distinguish between "open" and "closed" custodial placements for delinquents. In any case, the Young Offenders Act has clearly introduced new dynamics into the negotiated order among youth-processing organizations.

Cross-sectional studies can usually identify how initiatives such as the Young Offenders Act have affected the disposition of clients; only local studies, however, can clarify the dynamics that underlie these outcomes. Although the so-called evils of discretion and pragmatic considerations seem inescapable, our study suggests that control over admissions is the real issue underlying the failure of public policies. Policy makers should therefore examine the close link between control over admissions and the ability of organizations to skim clients off the top, thereby escalating the definition of their problems. Indeed, the notion that private institutions necessarily have more control over admissions than public ones needs to be reexamined from this viewpoint. As our study shows, the failure of The Boys' Farm, as a private institution, to control admissions and its subsequent ability, as a public one, to gain control of admissions were not related to the status of the institution *per se*. Instead, its failure was related as much to the kind of contract it had with the province – could the court control admissions? – and to the fact that other private children's institutions avoided such contracts. Although becoming a public institution in a regulated environment still involved contracts, these contracts were less meaningful in surroundings that permitted undetected case-by-case control over admissions.

Interorganizational contracts may well provide information about an organization's ability to control admissions, but the actual disposition of clients is determined by the way in which the organization actually uses these contracts. For example, in our study, the early juvenile court insisted on its contractual control over admissions, although later the director of youth protection and the social service centre did not. Insofar as contracts specify broad categories of clients, however, they can be circumvented in an environment that attaches more value to a case-by-case evaluation of clients than to the exercise of formal authority. Hence, it is the dichotomy between private and public institutions, regarding control over admissions, that should be reexamined: private programs with contractual control over admissions may well have less control than either public or private programs without contracts. Indeed, although private institutions have contracts that make their control or lack of control over admissions more obvious (see Guarino-Ghezzi and Byrne 1989), our study shows that public institutions are also actively engaged in the selection of clients (see also Messinger 1978). These processes can be quite covert: such client-selection strategies as those directly observed by Teram during the early 1980s, for example, do not leave the same traces as those that permitted Rains to discover client-recruitment strategies from the past.

Formal policies are subverted not only by these covert processes, but also by the allocation of resources. Here it is useful to distinguish between resources such as counselling services, or foster homes, that are designated for milder cases at the "soft end" of the youth-in-trouble system; and resources such as locked security units, that are designated for more serious cases at the "hard end" of the youth-in-trouble system. The "soft end" of the youth-in-trouble system is particularly prone to underfunding, because of notions claiming, for example, that "counselling services have an unlimited capacity to absorb new clients." The "hard end" of the system is less likely to be underfunded, because clients for secure custody appear to be more of a risk to the community than the clients on the waiting lists of overloaded caseworkers – a point that is often exploited by those looking for funds. Moreover, although overloaded caseworkers and soft-end programs can control the composition of their client populations by escalating undesirable clients, hard-end programs must expand their dumping ground, or look for even harder alternatives.

If professionals define client problems to fit the availability of resources, policy makers should be aware of the consequences of underfunding at the soft end of the youth-in-trouble system. In other words, the resources that are allocated when implementing the new delinquency policies oriented to accountability on the one hand, and diversion on the other, that will determine which goals take precedence. Under current conditions and practices, and if early trends toward increased rates of custody are any indication (Hackler 1987; Leschied and Jaffe 1988; Markwart and Corrado 1989), the commitment of Canada's new Young Offenders Act to criminalization is likely to take precedence.

Appendix

METHODS OF THE TWO STUDIES

The Historical Case Study – Prue Rains

I was drawn to study the history of The Boys' Farm because of my interest in youth-processing institutions (Rains 1971). As important were the critical histories of social control institutions that became salient for sociologists in the 1970s (Platt 1969; Rothman 1971; Foucault 1977; Ignatieff 1978; Rothman 1980), as well as the chance discovery of a wealth of primary material in two attics in the administration building at the original site of The Boys' Farm and Training School (in Prevost, formerly Shawbridge).[1]

With a temporary office at the Montreal headquarters of Shawbridge Youth Centres and a research assistant, I spent the spring and summer of 1983 (and several visits since) sorting through unending boxes, and assorted filing cabinets and piles of old papers and taking notes. Eventually, I photocopied much of this unorganized material.

The Boys' Farm material included the minutes of board of directors meetings from 1907 to 1970; scrapbooks of clippings from Montreal newspapers after 1920; minutes of the administration committee; internal reports, memos and correspondence of the superintendents, executive directors, and board of directors members; correspondence between these administrators and judges at the Montreal Social Welfare Court and Province of Quebec ministry officials; the three studies of The Boys' Farm carried out in the mid-1960s (the Caplan-Marcilio report 1966, the Shamsie report 1967, the Clendenen report 1967); and The Boys' Farm annual reports from 1910 to 1971. The minutes of the administration committee (a subcommittee of the board of directors which, with the superintendent and secretary-treasurer, dealt with the practical affairs of The Boys' Farm and made recommendations to the board) were especially valuable; not only were they more numerous and detailed than the minutes of the board of directors' meetings, they were also a great deal more candid than the annual reports. Annual reports were nonetheless useful as a source of quantitative admissions data.

The practices for reporting both qualitative and quantitative records were strikingly consistent over long spans of time because the records were kept from 1921 to 1941 by one man, Owen Dawson, and then, until 1966, by the successor he trained. Dawson's involvement with The Boys' Farm began when he became a member of the board of directors in 1911, ending with his death in 1955. In 1908, he founded the Griffintown Club (a boy's club in a Montreal slum), before working from 1912 to 1918 as assistant to the judge at the new Montreal Juvenile Court. He became secretary-treasurer of The Boys' Farm in 1921, managing director in 1936, and continued to serve on the administration committee and board of directors even after his retirement in 1941. Despite his long involvement and assiduously assembled records and scrapbooks, his own book about The Boys' Farm is remarkably bland – no doubt because he was, in his own words, "very sensitive with regard to hurting the feelings of people and never [did] so intentionally" (Dawson 1952, viii). William F. Shepherd, trained as Dawson's assistant in 1940, kept records from 1941 to 1966 – first as secretary-treasurer, then as executive director, of The Boys' Farm. His unpublished thesis on the history of the Montreal Council of Social Agencies (Shepherd 1957), written for McGill's School of Social Work while on leave, was one of several that contributed useful material on the development of Montreal's anglophone child-welfare system (Aiken 1950; Chan et al 1957; Douglas 1967; Mendelsohn and Ronald 1969; Thompson 1950) and The Boys' Farm (Mayotte 1949; Nearing 1945).

The Boys' Farm material and the issues it raised led me to look for archival material from Montreal's other anglophone youth-processing institutions. Having obtained permission from the Youth Horizons Foundation[2] to look at the Weredale House and Summerhill Homes Archives[3] at the National Archives in Ottawa, I found unpublished Montreal Council of Social Agency surveys, in addition to other material about child-welfare organizations – including Red Feather Year Books from 1958 through 1966 – at McGill University libraries and in the Weredale House Archives.[4] The chart prepared for Alliance Quebec by Allison and Prosser (1983) was also useful in tracing child welfare agencies through various name changes and amalgamations. Although I also found material concerning the anglophone juvenile-court clinic (created as the Child and Family Clinic in 1965) at the Douglas Hospital (Verdun), in annual reports from 1965 to 1973, I could find no systematic source of data for the Montreal Juvenile Court itself.

The Province of Quebec provided several rich sources of material: *Sessional Papers* (Penal Establishments), *Statistical Yearbooks* (Statistics of Reformatory Institutions and Statistics of Penal Institutions), and the reports of provincial commissions and special committees on social insurance (the Montpetit report, Quebec 1932), public assistance (the Boucher report, Quebec 1963), crime and the administration of justice (the Prevost report, Quebec 1970), health and social welfare (the Castonguay-Nepveu reports, Quebec 1967–72), children and adolescents placed in reception centres (the Batshaw report, Quebec 1976), and youth protection (the Charbonneau report, Quebec 1982). The full specifications are listed, by date, in the Bibliography, under "Quebec, Government of." Useful reviews of the development of provincial child-welfare structures and policies can be found in the Boucher report (Quebec 1963: 27–45, 153–58) and in part four (Social Services) of the Castonguay-Nepveu report (Quebec 1967–72, vol. 6, tome 1, 38–62).

The reports from Canada's royal commission on the penal system (Archambault report, Canada 1938) and the Department of Justice's committee on juvenile delinquency (Canada 1965) both proved useful in situating some issues (the age-extension issue, private agency control over admissions) within a broader Canadian context.

Finally, in an effort to overcome the handicaps of my training as a sociologist rather than an historian, and of my background as an American immigrant to Quebec and Canada, I have relied on secondary sources to understand the rise and fall of the clerical influence, and the shifts in provincial-federal relations – both of these having had a particular bearing on child-welfare policies in Quebec (Vigod 1986; Behiels 1985; Mongeau 1967; McRoberts 1988; Renaud 1976; Lesemann 1984).

The Qualitative Case Study – Eli Teram

My study originated from an interest in comparing the interorganizational relationships of workers at different hierarchical levels in human service organizations. The research was designed to remedy the methodological and substantive shortcomings impeding systematic investigation of this issue: the methodological reliance on quantitative data from managers; and the absence of a substantive focus on clients and those working directly with clients. I was interested, therefore, in studying a social service network that would provide opportunities to observe interorganizational relationships at several organizational levels. Montreal's anglophone youth-protection network was a good arena for such observations and its administrators generously allowed me access to relevant meetings and documents.

Given the state of interorganizational theory, a research design oriented towards formulating and verifying hypotheses would have been premature. Drawing on my social work experience and the work of open systems and contingency theorists, I could have formulated hypotheses involving the distinct functions of workers at different levels, their motivations for interacting with other organizations, and the substance and frequency of these exchanges. But I wanted to extend existing organizational theory and the "local wisdom" of social service workers and managers (Hackler 1983–84) by exploring how differences in interorganizational relations emerge and get handled.

To understand these processes I had to "go directly to the social world itself and attempt to uncover what people are up to at any given time in differing contexts" (Van Maanen 1983, 263). What I needed was a process-oriented approach that

would deal with changes in the underpinnings, in the infrastructure upon which the organization is built. This would involve attending to the micro-processes continuously occurring within the organization and its environment within a particular period of time, that is, the ongoing interactions that continuously reproduce the organization and/or alter it. It would also involve examining the transformation of context involved in major historical breaks. (Benson 1977, 11)

The basic postulate of a process analysis applied to the study of interorganizational relations is that "all systems structure and regulate themselves around the power relations established between their members and their units" (Crozier and Thoenig 1976). Such an analysis is not based on the measurement of resources controlled by interacting members or units, but on a qualitative assessment of the actions open to partners and the dynamics of their tactics in relation to their resources. Once the advantages of a qualitative approach became clear, it also became clear that participant observation was the most appropriate way of collecting the kind of information I needed.

I also chose participant observation because I needed information about issues that were potentially too sensitive to be provided without censorship or unintended distortion. It is widely recognized that, because informants may, when interviewed, be unwilling or even unable to talk about many issues of interest to the researcher, participant observation is one way of overcoming this problem (Becker and Geer 1957). Although interviews can elicit the "local wisdom" useful for understanding the dynamics of complex processes (Hackler 1983–84), researchers must first have some direct knowledge of the practices informants are being asked to explain. This direct knowledge is particularly important when informants are likely to employ "accounts"; that is, linguistic devices that "prevent conflicts from arising by verbally bridging the gap between action and expectations" (Scott and Lyman 1968, 46). Not knowing where these gaps lie, the researcher risks upsetting the interviewee by inadvertently confronting informants with "inappropriate" and seemingly rude questions. Participant observation accordingly prepares the ground for subsequent interviews, since "the independent evidence given by others may add to our direct experience, but only to the extent we have reason to believe, based ultimately on experience, that they are telling the truth, something which depends also in good part upon our knowing what their experience is" (Douglas 1976, 7).

With the benefit of hindsight, it is also now obvious that participant observation generated data that could not have been collected otherwise, and which, in turn, provided the basis for the analysis presented in chapters 6 through 8.

Field Work Sites. The field work (participant observation supplemented with informal interviews and organizational documents) was conducted at three points in time: during a three-month period in 1980, an eight-month period in 1981, and a two-month period in 1982. I observed settings that involved interorganizational relations at the institutional, managerial, and service staff levels.

At the institutional level, I observed meetings of the regional advisory committee, at which high-level institutional representatives from reception centres and social service centres (along with an informal representative from the psychiatric network) met to discuss policies and resource planning for the network.

At the managerial level, I observed three types of meetings:

• *network table meetings*, at which management representatives from the reception centres and the social service centre's department of youth protection met to deal with ongoing problems in the network;
• *parity committees meetings*, at which management representatives from each of the three reception centres[5] met separately with

management representatives from the social service centre to deal with contractual agreements between the social service centre and the reception centre; these committees met every month when contract renewals were imminent and less often after a contract was signed; and

• *joint-admissions committee meetings*: the organizational structure of the joint-admissions committee changed twice over the course of my field work, allowing me to compare

a. *centralized committee meetings*, at which managerial and social work staff from the social service centre met with managerial representatives from the reception centres and psychiatric network to negotiate client placements;

b. *decentralized committees meetings*, at which managerial and case-work staff from each of the three area social-service centres met with a single reception centre manager who, officially, represented the central-admissions committee but, unofficially, represented the reception centre;

c. *recentralized committee meetings*, at which the centralized structure was restored but without representation from the social work staff of the social service centre.

(The implications of these changes in the structure of the joint-admissions committee are analyzed in the third section of the book.)

At the lowest organizational level, where social workers directly involved with clients dealt with one another in intraorganizational and interorganizational staff meetings, I again observed three types of meetings:

• *reception centre team meetings* at Youth Horizons; team meetings included child-care workers from the reception-centre, and their supervisors, and social workers from the social service centre;

• *youth-protection-team table meetings*, an intraorganizational meeting within the social service centre, where staff members from the department of youth protection, the resource development division, court units, and area social-service centres, along with a rotating case-review analyst and the chairperson of the central admissions committee, discussed procedures and guidelines for implementing the Youth Protection Act;

• *reception centre staff meetings* at Shawbridge Youth Centres, at which social workers from the reception centre met with their supervisor, as a group, to discuss organizational issues affecting their work.

I also attended a variety of other meetings, including meetings between individual social workers and case conferences.

Data differences.   There were fundamental differences between the data collected through observations and informal interviews. Observations netted me news about "the way things are"; informal interviews netted me news about the "accounts" people give as representatives of their organization. For example, social workers from the reception centre used staff meetings as a forum for raising questions and pointing out problems. Because they wanted their concerns to be heard and dealt with, they presented their difficulties in stark terms to make a point. When interviewed, however, they emphasized the positive aspects of the reception centre, sometimes qualifying statements made in staff meetings, and sometimes defending policies they had questioned in staff meetings.

A second issue related to the comparison between observations and informal interviews has to do with how I was perceived, especially when observing the joint-admissions committees. Because I attended committee meetings regularly, referring social workers tended to identify me with the committee; that may explain why they were reluctant to discuss their reactions to the committee's response to their client referral. I therefore had subsequent talks with these workers, primarily to confirm my observation about what happened to their client rather than to explore how they felt about it.

I also have abundant evidence that observations are more reliable than documents. Many times, for instance, the short minutes of committee meetings did not represent what actually transpired in meetings; they included the statement of problems and proposed solutions but omitted the interactions that led to these solutions. (Along these same lines, Prue Rains also found publicly accessible minutes of annual board meetings a great deal less informative – except as a source of statistics – than the minutes of more private meetings, and these, in turn, less informative than internal memos, reports and correspondence.)

Notes

1 "Net-widening" occurs when reforms, designed as *substitutes* for incarceration or court adjudication, instead become *supplements* to the social control system, thus "widening the net of social control" (Cohen 1979 a,b). Net-widening has been identified as an effect not just of juvenile justice reforms, but of criminal justice reforms more generally (Austin and Krisberg 1981; Cohen 1985, 43–56). For example, Rothman (1980, 110–13) contends that the invention of probation widened the net because judges used it as a tougher alternative to suspended sentences, rather than as a more lenient substitute for incarceration.

2 "Transcarceration" occurs when reforms designed to take or keep people out of institutions instead simply shift these people to different kinds of institutions: from public to private institutions, from mental to correctional institutions, from correctional to child-welfare or mental health institutions. Studies that identify these unintended shifts of adults or youths from one social control system to another have also referred to the same phenomenon in their discussions of "transinstitutionalization" (Warren 1981), "relabelling" (Van Dusen 1981), and "new nets" (Austin and Krisberg 1981).

3 The welfare-oriented approach broadened the definition of delinquency to include "status" offences: offences that are 'crimes' for children but not adults, such as drinking, truancy, incorrigibility, promiscuity, and running away from home.

4 Some argue, however, that the Toronto data do not demonstrate reduced incarceration (West 1984, 44; Rains 1984).

5 For useful reviews of studies that evaluate such reforms, see Klein (1979) and Moyer (1980).

6 Rooke and Schnell's (1983) history of the rise and fall of the "Protestant orphan's home" in English Canada describes early orphanages as the first specialized institutions for children. The practice of foster-home placement thus "respecialized" these institutions as places for marginal rather than normal children.

7 Lerman's study, which covers roughly sixty years up to the mid-1970s, employs official sources of data on the incarceration of delinquent, neglected, and emotionally disturbed youths for the United States as a whole, and controls for demographic changes in the size of the youth population.

8 In this connection, Polk (1987, 376) has argued that expanded state control in the form of net-widening was an *intended* effect of diversion policies, "a logical consequence of the ideas within which the programs were initially conceived and defined," because "the persons who controlled the implementation of these efforts ... were explicitly – and from the beginning – in the business of expanding the treatment or rehabilitative resources of the community."

9 When the qualifications in question are negative (such as "psychiatric disturbances" or "delinquent behaviour"), organizations usually prefer clients who have less serious problems than the organization is mandated for and funded to serve. When the qualifications in question are positive (such as higher levels of education or IQ), organizations usually prefer better qualified clients than they are supposed to serve.

10 These included two reform schools run by Catholic orders for francophone delinquent boys and girls, a reform school for anglophone delinquent girls, and The Boys' Farm – the only reform school for anglophone delinquent boys.

11 The revisionist view suggests that the juvenile court was not a benevolent reform but an extension of state control over working-class families – and thus unlikely to "decarcerate" youth.

12 In Quebec, however, the emergence of a youth-in-trouble system was not accomplished through the expansion of private institutions, as occurred in the United States. It was the result of a policy intended to diffuse the boundaries between child-welfare and delinquency programs.

13 The Young Offenders Act was passed in the Canadian House of Commons in July 1982, and went into effect in April 1984.

PART ONE: INTRODUCTION

1 *An Act for Establishing Prisons for Young Offenders*, 20 Vic., 1857, c. 28.
2 Two reformatories were established, one in Upper Canada at Penetanguishene, the other in Lower Canada at Isle aux Noix.

3 Industrial schools "differed from the reformatory in structure, clientele and sentencing provisions" (Jones 1978, 234); they accepted younger children, on indeterminate sentences, and housed them in smaller "cottages" staffed by houseparents.

4 Industrial schools were designed initially for neglected, rather than delinquent or dependent, youths. Pointing out that child-savers of the time often lumped "neglected," "dependent," and "delinquent" children together, Sutherland (1976, 97–8) provides useful distinctions: neglected children were the street children under the age of fourteen (beggars, newsboys, waifs, strays, vagrants) of new concern to mid-Victorians (Houston 1972, 1982). Dependent children were those without families (foundlings, orphans). Delinquent children broke laws.

5 Known for many years as the Montreal Reformatory for Boys, Mont St-Antoine contracted with the Province of Quebec under the "Loi des écoles d'industries, S.Q. 1869, c. 17" to accept boys convicted and sentenced of crimes by adult courts.

6 The Frères de la charité, a Belgian order, had experience in reformatory work and may have been recruited to Quebec for this reason (Copp 1974; Tremblay 1984).

7 J.S. Buchan, quoted in the Boys' Home annual report, 1908. The Boys' Home was founded in 1870 as a supervised alternative to public boarding houses for young working boys. The most complete collection of archival materials for the Boys' Home, later called Weredale House, can be found in the Weredale House Archives (see Bibliography).

8 In 1943, this theme was still emphasized in retelling how the first fifteen boys had arrived: "The burly guards who brought the lads from Sherbrooke jail had them all hand-cuffed together, and when they saw the place at Shawbridge, and found half the staff were women, they almost refused to leave the boys there, believing they could not be left alone unless they were securely locked behind bars. The next morning all the boys were still there and after thirty-five years, the same 'open-door' policy is in force and there are still no cells or iron bars at the Farm" (from an address given by a Boys' Farm staff member, quoted in Nearing 1945, 1–2).

9 Copp (1974, 112, 113) observes that The Boys' Farm embodied "one of the most popular notions about reformatories – the idea that they should be located in the country and the children taught to farm"; and he points out that there was "a certain irony in the decision of the Anglo-Protestant community to embrace the land as a curative while French Canadian delinquents were prepared for life in the city."

10 Visiting for the first time in 1924, Judge L.O. Lacroix of the Montreal juvenile court told a reporter, "It is not like a reformatory, it is more like

a boarding college, and it impressed me very much" (*Montreal Star*, 22 November 1924).

11 Details from J.J.E. Woods' report as provincial inspector of reformatories (Quebec, *Sessional Paper* no. 20, 1909–10) and Dawson 1952.

12 Kelso – "the legendary father of the Canadian child welfare movement" (Harevan 1969, 86) – was a Toronto journalist whose moving editorials aroused public interest in neglected and delinquent children. "In 1891 Kelso mobilized public support for the founding of the Toronto Children's Aid Society, modeled after the New York Children's Aid Society. From its inception, however, its goals and prescribed functions exceeded those of the New York Society: the establishment of a children's shelter, separate trials of juvenile offenders, the appointment of a probation officer for the court" (Harevan 1969, 87). Kelso became Ontario's superintendent of neglected and dependent children in 1893 and contributed to the formation of twenty-nine children's aid societies across the province (Sutherland 1976, 112–15). When the Ontario Reformatory for Boys at Penetanguishene shut down in 1904, Kelso took on the foster home placement of its delinquent boys as a demonstration project (Jones 1978). Kelso maintained wide contacts in Canada and the United States with child-savers, including those involved in the juvenile court movement (Harevan 1969; Sutherland 1976, 119–23; Hagan and Leon 1977).

13 Kelso, who "acted as a personal link between Canada and the United States" (Harevan 1969, 86), had met key activists in the American juvenile court movement (Chicago's Harvey B. Hurd, first judge of the Chicago Juvenile Court in 1899, and Denver's Judge Lindsey in 1906). "In 1906 Kelso drafted a provincial law, which he patterned on the Illinois Act" (Harevan 1969, 89).

14 Following his attendance at the National Conference Of Charities and Correction in Philadelphia in 1906, W.L. Scott, lawyer and president of the Ottawa Children's Aid Society, adapted Philadelphia's probation system for Ottawa's use. But "since probation officers had no legal status, they were unable to gain admission into homes where they were not welcomed" (Sutherland 1976, 120). In an effort to solve this problem, Scott drafted and promoted the Juvenile Delinquents Act, with help from his father, Senator R.W. Scott, and Senator F.L. Beique. Sutherland (1976, 122) contends: "In enacting the statute, the federal government was clearly responding to the immediate, practical needs of the Ottawa Children's Aid Society."

15 It is clear that, as an author and prime promoter of the legislation, W.L. Scott intended a broad, rather than narrow, reading of delinquent offences. Commenting on the 1924 addition of "sexual immorality or any similar form of vice" to the list of delinquent offences,

Scott says, "It has sometimes been suggested that other specific acts should be added to this definition of a 'juvenile delinquent', but I think that this would be unwise. The definition, it seems to me, is extremely wide, and *to add further specific acts to it might possibly result in narrowing the meaning of the general words.*" (Scott 1930, 9; emphasis added.)

16 Early versions of a juvenile court existed in Toronto, where separate children's sessions had been held since 1894, and in Ottawa, where two probation officers were supplied to the separate children's court in 1906. Some people claim that the Toronto court precedes the first American courts in Chicago (1898) and Denver (1899), which opened "largely through the information supplied and the initiative given in the Toronto experiment" (MacGill 1925, 23). As Hagan and Leon (1977, 592) observe, Kelso's claims "are less important for their factual accuracy than for their indication of close connections between Canadian and American child-saving efforts."

17 Commenting specifically on the Montreal juvenile court (as we shall usually call it), Scott (1930, 38) complains: "It seems a pity that the court was not called 'The Juvenile Court', the name by which it is now universally known, instead of 'The Juvenile Delinquents Court.'" Scott, as chair of the Ottawa Children's Aid Society and author of the Juvenile Delinquents Act, had elicited support in Montreal for the establishment of juvenile courts at a public meeting in 1907. On 4 June 1910, the Province of Quebec established a court of record called "The Juvenile Delinquents' Court" in and for the City of Montreal. Following negotiations between the province and the city, the act was enforced on 26 December 1911, and the court opened officially on 22 March 1912, in what had been a private house on Champs de Mars Street. The court moved to its current location on St-Denis Street in 1932 (Mendelsohn and Ronald 1969).

18 By 1942, there were three judges: Judges Robillard and Laramee, who were both francophones, and Judge Nicholson, who was the first anglophone judge (Canadian Welfare Council 1942).

19 The Montreal Children's Aid Society, formed in 1907 following Scott's visit, promoted probation as early as 1908. It appears to have become the Montreal Juvenile Court Committee – a Protestant committee that maintained close association with the probation officers and their work, and advised the court on the disposition of cases (Mendelsohn and Ronald 1969, 20–1, 30–1). By 1942, there were two juvenile-court committees – one Protestant, one Jewish. The committees, including a later "French Committee," were rendered increasingly superfluous by the "rise of the professional worker" and suspended operation in 1951 (Mendolsohn and Ronald 1969, 103).

20 The 1914 report listed 39 offenses in the order of their frequency. The front runners were: theft (497), vagrancy (190), deserting home (44), disobedience (40), damaging property (38), being neglected or abandoned children (34), breaking into a store (22), selling papers without a licence (22), breaking into houses (18), incorrigibility (16), selling of papers after 9:30 A.M. (10) ... (Quebec, *Sessional Papers*, 1914)

21 For archival information on this institution, see Girls' Cottage School in Bibliography.

CHAPTER TWO

1 Montreal contained the province's only juvenile court until 1940 and its largest reform-school population. The operations of the Montreal court thus account for most, although not all, of the commitments to provincial institutions.

2 I could not find systematic data from the Montreal juvenile court's early years. The clerk of court's reports for 1914 and 1915 (Quebec, *Sessional Papers*, 1914, 1915) suggest that probation was a favoured disposition from the start. In 1914 and 1915, 819 and 802 delinquents, respectively, were "let out on trial," while 156 and 159 were sent to reform schools.

3 The board, during the 1920s, was composed of men who headed, or worked at the top level of, their respective enterprises: E.W. Beatty, Canadian Pacific Railway; J.W. McConnell, St. Lawrence Sugar Refineries and the *Montreal Star*; F.B. Whittet, Riorden Pulp and Paper; N.L.C. Mather, National City Investment Bankers; A.D. MacTier, Canadian Pacific Railway; C.E. Neill, Royal Bank of Canada; Lyon Cohen, coal merchants and dredging contractors, brass founders, and export clothiers companies; Walter Mitchell, provincial treasurer, Quebec minister of Municipal Affairs, Liberal member of the federal House of Commons, chairman of the provincial Protestant Committee of the Council of Education, and head of a law firm; A.A. Magee, partner in a law firm; and J.H. Birks, owner of Henry Birks & Sons, a jewellry store. All were of sufficient prominence to be listed in *Who's Who in Canada*. Beatty served as board president until 1942.

4 The province negotiated its financial arrangements independently with each reform school (there were five, including The Boys' Farm). The per capita cost for clients at The Boys' Farm consistently ran much higher than those of keeping clients at the province's French reform schools, largely because the latter were supported and staffed by religious orders. It seems reasonable to suppose that the province preferred to give The Boys' Farm special annual grants rather than to raise its per diem, thereby avoiding the establishment of a precedent for its dealings with other reform schools.

5 Eight months later, the reporter went on to explain, Mrs. Fawns (she used her remarried name) was outraged to discover her twelve-year-old son had been flogged with a hose. "I stood it for a while ... because I thought these people must know what they were doing, as they are all educated people and supposed to be ladies and gentlemen ... But when I went there last Sunday, things were too much ... So I lost my temper and went after them. And I'm going to keep after them until I get my boy out of there. That's all. I can't stomach the idea of those people beating my child" (*Montreal Star* 1923b).

6 The active recruitment of voluntary clients was considered again when juvenile court commitments dropped seriously following the Second World War. During The Boys' Farm's second major population crisis (1946–49), its executive director wrote to a board member: "With the increase in costs we should, I believe, increase our rates for voluntary students which will have the effect, I would think, of discouraging placements so that we can hardly expect to increase our population by attempting to add to the number of voluntary pupils. They must, and should, come from the agencies and magistrates who deal with difficult children" (BFTS, internal correspondence, letter dated 20 January 1948). The number of voluntary cases at the reform school declined, and none were reported after 1957.

7 It may seem odd that the board of directors first approached executive, rather than legal or judicial, authorities about implementing indefinite sentences. Eventually, however, the board did seek a legal interpretation of the Juvenile Delinquents Act (1908). But because the act was federal legislation enacted provincially by executive proclamation, there was some ambiguity as to which authority was responsible for its interpretation. The board's initial approach also reflected its own contacts and prior experience with provincial authorities about institutional matters, which had customarily been handled by the provincial secretary.

8 These shorter sentences, when served in detention centers rather than reform schools, also decreased the populations of the reform schools. Schlossman (1977, 155) observes: "While the juvenile court sent relatively few children to reformatories, it held large numbers on short-term sentences in the detention center before, during, and sometimes after trial." In the absence of adequate detention facilities, the Montreal court held both French-speaking and English-speaking boys at the Montreal Reformatory (the French reform school for boys also known as Mont St Antoine). The large number of boys held there "provisionally for inquiry" suggests that, during the 1920s, the Montreal court used short-term detention in much the same way – that is, as an alternative to outright commitment to reform schools.

9 Although The Boys' Farm eventually established procedures for allocating parole, as well as a committee that reviewed boys for parole, that
did not occur until the 1940s, when the Farm had acquired control over
the release date of boys (even then, the control was limited by the definite sentence). The plan to establish a "parole board" in 1924 was therefore something of a rhetorical device, designed to express a form of
control over sentences that The Boys' Farm hoped for but did not have.

10 The Montreal juvenile court did not make routine use of the indefinite
sentence until the early 1950s. But, by then, the duration of the usual
indefinite sentence was between fifteen and eighteen months, with a
review required after the first twelve months. In other words, shorter
indefinite terms had replaced longer definite terms. Indeed, in the mid-
1960s, declining sentence lengths were contributing to The Boys' Farm's
most serious population crisis. By then, as demonstrated in chapter 3,
the reform school was most concerned with the *kinds* of boys being sent
(and not sent) by the court; they chose not to oppose shorter sentences
for fear of ruling out the commitment of younger, less "hard-core"
delinquent boys.   .

11 Schlossman (1977, 232), however, contends that Platt's claims are not
supported by his data: "The statistical evidence he offers to support his
contention, pp. 140–1, in no way does so because he does not compare
the situation before and after the establishment of the juvenile court."

12 Hagan and Leon (1977) note the extensive use made of both formal and
informal probation by the early Toronto court, and "argue that, contrary
to Platt's claim, there is no evidence that the number of incarcerated
juveniles increased, as they found that 123 Toronto youngsters were
imprisoned in 1911 (the year before the Toronto court opened), while
only 85 were institutionalized in 1912" (West 1984, 44). Yet, as West
observes, their own "ambiguous Toronto data" appears to include children removed from their homes and placed in institutions but not
counted as "institutionalized."

13 Their data skip from 1912 to 1920.

14 In this connection, a 1947 study of The Boys' Farm observes: "There are
other boys in the school too who are more neglected than delinquent
children. Parents have been known to have their boy or boys committed to Shawbridge because they could not or would not look after
them. We all know that the war has placed many children almost completely on their own initiative. One lad told us that his brother and two
sisters had been placed away from home. The father was overseas and
the mother was holding a job in a munitions plant. Whether this is a
result of income inadequacies or misinterpretation of the responsibilities
of parenthood we are not prepared to say" (Nearing 1945, 20).

15 The striking use made of both formal and informal probation by the new Toronto juvenile court in 1912 was clearly the legacy of ideas and structures already set into place by J.J. Kelso's activism. Hagan and Leon (1977) note, of course, the great potential for informal control provided by effective probation supervision of children and their families.

16 In 1924, E.W. Beatty, president of the Canadian Pacific Railway and of The Boys' Farm, addressed the Toronto Social Service Committee about the proposed Boys' Home to be built by the Ontario government: "If I might offer a suggestion it would be that the Government should call for and receive the active assistance of men in business life, who should bring to bear upon the administration the results of their wide business experience and give also by their occasional presence at the Farm an inspiration due to personal contact, which I am convinced is one of the most powerful influences in the development of any boy's character." In this sense, Beatty and other prominent men offered themselves as role models, as examples of "the inexpressible glory of achievement through personal effort" (*Gazette*, 6 April 1924).

17 The recruitment of Walter Mitchell, provincial treasurer from 1914 to 1921, to The Boys' Farm's board of directors in 1923, underlines the ties that linked Montreal's English business elite, the provincial government and The Boys' Farm.

CHAPTER THREE

1 The term "reform school" is used generically and includes industrial schools. Reform schools in Ontario and Quebec were designated officially as industrial schools.

2 As the result of legislation in 1908, English courts could sentence young offenders between the ages of sixteen and twenty-one to a Borstal institution for one to three years, rather than to ordinary penal institutions.

3 In 1943, school attendance for children between the ages of six and fourteen became compulsory in Quebec.

4 Even now the main way of returning to Montreal is to hitchhike on the nearby highway, a conspicuous action in a small town.

5 On 13 April 1909, "two boys attempted to escape by walking on the railway, but were captured" five miles away. The superintendent made an example of this first runaway attempt by "inflicting corporal punishment by means of a strap in presence of the whole staff who were assembled as witnesses, and placed the offenders on an allowance of bread and water for some days" (BFTS, board minutes, Report to The Boys' Home board of directors from the chairman, J.S. Buchan, 14 May 1909).

6 Major Ralph Willcock had been "second in command of the 42nd battalion during the First World War." He was recruited to The Boys' Farm in 1928 from Wolfville, Nova Scotia, where he had been house master at Horton Academy. He left in 1942 to do war work (Dawson 1952).

7 "During the years of World War II, the boy population of the School rose as high as two hundred and fifty. At that time building materials were scarce and every available space was used to house the residents." Two new cottages were constructed during 1945, bringing the total to six cottages "planned to house about thirty boys with a married couple as cottage parents. Each cottage has a large dormitory on the second floor and there are showers and locker rooms in their basements. All meals are served in the large dining room in the central administration building" (Mayotte 1949, 18–24).

8 It is not surprising that boys were homesick, for the rules only permitted relatives (not more than two) to visit once a month (Nearing 1945, 71).

9 The departing superintendent, Howard Mandigo (1943–45), resigned to take up farming in Vermont. He had served as assistant to Superintendent Barss, had left to take charge of the St. John's Industrial School in New Brunswick, and had returned to replace Major Willcock in 1943 (Dawson 1952).

10 George Young returned to his ministerial work in Marmora, Ontario, after two-and-a-half years at The Boys' Farm.

11 The author of this response to Superintendent Young's "Memorandum re Detention Facilities at The Boys' Farm" was Col. Allan A. Magee, QC, OBE, of Magee and O'Donnell, Advocates, Barristers etc. He served as president of The Boys' Farm's board of directors from 1942–45, and continued to serve on the board for more than ten years. He was succeeded as board president by Walter P. Zeller (1945–47 and 1951–57) and William Harrison (1947–50). Most board members served for many years in various capacities; for example, as members of the administration and finance committees (Dawson, 1952).

12 These now included Boscoville, a showcase facility for francophone delinquent boys founded officially in 1954. Arising from work with delinquent boys that Père Albert Roger and Gilles Gendreau began in 1947, Boscoville was modelled originally on the work of Italian priest Don Jean Bosco and Father Flanagan's Boys Town in Omaha, Nebraska. Its development as a progressive "experiment" expressed its founders' continuing exploration of new educational theories and models in France, Belgium (Ovide Decroly), Holland, Germany, Switzerland (Piaget) and Italy. Boscoville did not lock boys up, and there were runaways (Rumilly 1978, 118–20).

13 After the new legislation in 1950, reform schools were called youth-protection schools, and the Montreal juvenile court was called the Montreal social welfare court. The former names are retained in this chapter for continuity.

14 Centre Berthelet opened its detention unit for delinquent boys in 1964: three cells were reserved for The Boys' Farm, seven allotted to other institutions, and the rest reserved to back up its own "open" observation units. From 1964–68, it seems to have provided backup placements primarily for Boscoville. Material on Centre Berthelet can be found in Laflamme-Cusson and Baril 1975, vol. 2: 185–89; in the Prevost report (Quebec 1970, vol. 4, tome 3: 307–21; and in the Batshaw report (Quebec 1976, tome 1: 526–49).

15 Before becoming cottage parents at The Boys' Farm in 1946, A.L. Evans and his wife were in charge of the Ladies' Benevolent Society orphanage for eighty small boys and girls. He became superintendent in 1948. Henri Joubrel, a visiting specialist from France, probably refers to Evans in his comments about The Boys' Farm in 1953: the place, he said, was "typically British, where a seventy-year-old educator and his sixty-year-old wife are the ones who succeed the best with children" (Rumilly 1978, 92; our translation).

16 There is evidence that boys sometimes ran away because they were beaten up by other boys. In October 1962, one boy "ran away approximately one-and-a-half hours after being allocated a cottage. He surrendered voluntarily and appeared before the judge and stated that he was not going to stay at The Boys' Farm and get beaten up" (BFTS, internal correspondence, Aldersley, 2 October 1962).

17 R. Lyman Williams used these words to support Superintendent Evans' new request in 1964 for a "maximum security room." Williams was, at the time, chairman of the administration committee, a post commonly held prior to becoming president of the board of directors – which he became in 1968. (BFTS, internal correspondence, Williams, 24 April, 1964, in a document marked "confidential").

18 Along these same lines, Bortner (1986, 57) points out, in his recent study of the remand of juveniles to adult court, that "a significant number of juveniles remanded to adult court are returned to the community immediately or shortly after conviction. The possible reasons for this are several. The chief ones include their first-time offender status in the adult system, the relatively minor nature of their offences, and the brevity of their offence histories *compared to adult offenders.*"

19 The Prisons and Reformatories Act constituted chapter 163 of the *Revised Statutes of Canada* of 1927 (Canada 1927). Following further consolidation of the federal statutes in 1952, the act became chapter 217 of the *Revised Statutes of Canada* of 1952.

20 In 1946, Judge Nicholson of the Montreal juvenile court requested the board of directors of The Boys' Farm to pass a resolution authorizing the superintendent and a spokesman for the board to make such requests. The board did so.

21 By 1956, boys were sent in this way to Bordeaux prison (for adults) or to the Federal Training Centre at the St-Vincent de Paul Penitentiary in Laval. A court probation officer favoured the construction of a "detention cottage" for runaways at The Boys' Farm, on the grounds that "no other alternative placement is possible besides Bordeaux or a long term at St Vincent de Paul. My own opinion is that this particular aspect cannot receive too much emphasis because of the shocking conditions existing in alternative places of confinement such as Bordeaux" (BFTS, external correspondence, Stevenson, 3 April 1956).

22 By this time, The Boys' Farm had acquired the right to determine the date of release within the terms of the indefinite sentence; this new court procedure, therefore, technically required The Boys' Farm to discharge the boy prior to his recommitment.

23 As noted in the previous chapter, shorter indefinite sentences had replaced longer definite sentences by the early 1950s.

24 John Weir was secretary-treasurer of The Boys' Farm.

25 Evans was superintendent at The Boys' Farm.

26 This population drop occurred despite: (1) increases in the number of eligible (in terms of age and language) boys in Montreal; (2) increases in the number of appearances of delinquent boys at the Montreal Social Welfare Court; and (3) the stability of sentence lengths after 1958.

27 After 1950, the client population at The Boys' Farm included youth-protection cases as well as delinquents. Youth-protection clients were younger. We have reported The Boys' Farm's concern regarding older boys, rather than the average age of its clients, because The Boys' Farm's "average" age included the younger protection cases.

28 In metropolitan Montreal, the number of boys between the ages of ten and nineteen increased across the census years 1951, 1961, and 1971. Although The Boys' Farm drew primarily on the non-French-speaking population, the number of both English-speakers and immigrants in metropolitan Montreal also increased from 1951 to 1971 (Statistics Canada, *Montreal*). In other words, the number of boys of reform-school age increased.

29 Although the number of appearances made by delinquent boys at the Montreal juvenile court did not keep pace with the increase of boys in the larger population, the number of appearances did not drop, except during 1963 and 1964. Moreover, the number of court appearances made by delinquent boys more than doubled from 1964 through 1970 (Statistics Canada, *Juvenile Delinquents*). These figures can be interpreted

as reflecting increases in delinquency, or increases in the official activities necessary to bring boys to court. Neither the census data, nor the court data are broken down more specifically by age.

30 Quotes from a document discussing a "temporary lock-up" by Lyman Williams, chairman of the administration committee (BFTS, internal correspondence, Williams, 24 April 1964). It also seems reasonable to speculate about the motives of the board members, as follows: board members gave their time to The Boys' Farm as a charitable activity, justified as an attempt to reform wayward boys. If they had solved their practical and financial problems by building locked units, they would have turned themselves into custodians of a juvenile prison, thereby undercutting the charitable rationale that justified their involvement.

31 While noting that corporal punishment "is not our general policy," Superintendent Evans reports on its use in a memorandum "Re: Corporal Punishment" (BFTS, internal correspondence, Evans, 26 August 1963): "During the past week and especially since the August leave period, we have had difficulties in managing boys because of serious misbehavior, misconduct, and AWOLS. Today a disciplinary court was held to clear up some of this disturbance and particularly because we had to deal with the return of 3 AWOLS at noon, followed by 5 more returns at 1:00 P.M. by court officers. Several boys were punished (corporal punishment) ... in the hope that it might prove helpful to them and especially act as a deterrent to others."

32 In his legally oriented discussion and comparison of Canada's old Juvenile Delinquents Act and new Young Offenders Act, Wilson (1982, 225–44) provides a critical discussion of this option. Peterson (1988) also reviews the literature on waivers from juvenile to adult courts in the context of New York State's reversed waiver option: there, sixteen- to eighteen-year-olds are defined as adults but can be granted youthful offender status and waived to juvenile courts. Peterson provides an analysis of how this discretion produces discriminatory sentencing patterns. In keeping with Needleman's (1981) cautionary remarks about the "discrepant assumptions" made about juvenile-court screening, Bortner's (1986) study of the remand of juveniles to adult court calls two such assumptions into question: that the remand process protects the community by incarcerating juveniles, and that juveniles are remanded because they are intractable or dangerous.

33 As Cohen (1985, 55) observes, "The disposition received by an offender arriving at a particular level is now affected by the knowledge that he was 'diverted' at an earlier level. The most severe punishments go not just to the worst offenders in legalistic terms, but to those who foul up at their previous levels."

34 In 1966, a confidential report to the board of directors from an external
consultant noted that "almost every boy admitted in January 1966 ran
away the next day" (BFTS, reports, Marcilio report, 1966).

PART TWO: INTRODUCTION

1 Useful reviews of the development of child welfare structures and policies by the Province of Quebec can be found in the Boucher report
(Quebec 1963: 27–45; 153–58) and in part four (Social Services) of the
Castonguay-Nepveu report (Quebec 1967–72, vol. 6, tome 1, 38–68).
2 Montreal was the primary focus of industrialization and urbanization in
the province; its population tripled to 618,500 between 1901 and 1921
(McRoberts 1988, 58).
3 Despite the controversy it provoked, passage of the Child Adoption Act
(1924) addressed the problem of overcrowded orphanages and found-
ling homes by providing the first legal basis for adoption (Vigod 1986,
115–17).
4 This was recommended by Quebec's Montpetit Commission on Social
Insurance (1930–32), which proposed many other progressive reforms
that were not implemented: establishment of a provincial youth-protection bureau, family allowances, health and unemployment insurance
(Mongeau 1967, 60–3). The commission's recommended assistance for
needy mothers was implemented in 1937.
   The Montreal Council of Social Agencies had long campaigned for
this extension of coverage to non-institutional agencies (Aiken 1950).
Thus, the act "was reinterpreted to recognize English-speaking Protestant, Catholic and Jewish charitable agencies, almost exclusively cen-
tered on home care, as institutions 'sans murs' eligible for small grants.
The French-speaking social service agencies only availed themselves of
this possibility some ten years later" (Johnston 1985, 195).
5 The Department of Health was, itself, created in 1936.
6 The jurisdiction of the Department of Social Welfare and Youth
included juvenile delinquents but not children's institutions and foster-
home placement agencies, until 1957 (Quebec 1967–72, Castonguay-
Nepveu report, Social Services, vol. 6, tome 1, 48). These charitable
institutions subsidized by the Public Charities Act remained under the
jurisdiction of the Department of Health.
7 Attached to the Montreal juvenile court, the Child Aid Clinic was, however, "forced to discontinue serving non-French-speaking children
because of increasing work loads and the unavailability of English-
speaking staff" (Mendelsohn and Ronald 1969, 53).
8 The Juvenile Delinquents Court of Montreal became the Social Welfare
Court of the Montreal Judicial District, while the "staff of the old

Juvenile Delinquents Court became the staff of the new Court" (Mendolsohn and Ronald 1969, 56).

9 For a presentation of the act's central features, see "Youth Protection Schools" in Quebec, *Statistical Year Book 1950*: 165–69.

10 Regarding amendments to the act in 1959–60, Montreal's social-welfare court judges nevertheless registered their objection to this usurpation of their formal placement authority (viewed by them as the executive assumption of judicial powers) at a meeting in December 1960 (Quebec 1970, vol. 4, tome 1: 651).

11 Listed in the order of their federation these were: the anglophone, Jewish, Federation of Jewish Philanthropies (1916); the anglophone, Protestant, Montreal Council of Social Agencies (1919); the anglophone, Catholic, Federation of Catholic Charities (1930); and the francophone, Catholic, Fédération des oeuvres de charité canadiennes-françaises (1932). (The Welfare Federation, formed in 1921, served as the fund-raising body for the Montreal Council of Social Agencies.) In 1941, the four federations established an Inter-Federation Council to favour joint action.

12 These were the Protestant Infant's Home (1869), the Protestant Orphan's Asylum (1820), and the Ladies Benevolent Society Home (1832); in addition, The Boys' Home (1870) provided a supervised alternative to public boarding houses for young working boys, and came to resemble an orphanage as the spread of schooling to older children transformed its population from working boys to dependent schoolboys.

13 John Howard Toynbee Falk, "the chief architect of the Council," was familiar with modern welfare developments in England, where he grew up and was educated, in the United States, and in Canada. Before arriving in Montreal to head the new School of Social Work at McGill University, he was director of boys' work at the Christodora House Settlement in New York City, then founder and head of the Winnipeg Associated Charities (Shepherd 1957, 47–51).

14 The Children's Bureau became eligible for provincial support as a non-institutional agency in 1930 (Aikin 1950, 127).

15 Carstens criticized Montreal's dependence on "congregate and unspecialized children's institutions under private (voluntary) management." He promoted the new policy of the New Haven Orphan Asylum as an alternative model: "The management of this institution does not believe in custodial institutional care for normal children. It does not believe in breaking up homes if that can be avoided" (Montreal Council of Social Agencies, Carstens report, 1924: 1,9).

16 Weredale House Archives, Memorandum "On the Question of Intake," 18 October 1950, NA, MG 28 I 405, vol. 5, file 7.

17 The Protestant Infant's Home became the Protestant Foster Home Centre in 1936, and eventually merged with the Children's Bureau as

the Children's Service Center (1951). The Ladies Benevolent Society shut down its orphanage in 1945, amalgamating with the Protestant Orphan's Asylum in 1946 to serve girls; this institution became known as Summerhill House. The Boys' Home, known as Weredale House after 1930, was the only surviving Protestant orphanage for boys.

18 This section is based on material for 1950 and 1951 from the Weredale House Archives, NA, MG 28, I 405, vol. 5, file 7 (Admission Policy – Correspondence, memoranda and reports, 1946–67). The file includes several lengthy memoranda "on the question of intake" cited by date.

19 Older boys were referred to Weredale House from a variety of sources: the Children's Bureau, the Family Welfare/Service Association, the Society for the Protection of Women and Children, the Protestant School Board Attendance Department, and parents.

20 In a resolution passed on 31 May 1950 and submitted to the Montreal Council of Social Agencies (also known as the Welfare Federation) on 10 June 1950, the Weredale House board of governors noted that "Weredale House is continuously operating between ten and fifteen boys below capacity, when it is our firm belief that the growth of the City alone indicates an increased need for the services we offer to dependent and neglected youth." On 14 June 1950, the Children's Aid Society board of directors meeting noted that: "Weredale House was alarmed because of an apparent shrinking number of children in care."

21 This was how the Children's Aid Society's board of directors character- ized their own convictions in reaction to complaints from Weredale House (Weredale House Archives, correspondence on the question of intake, 13 December 1950).

22 A memorandum prepared by the Weredale House board of governors "on the question of intake" states: "We are now firm in our belief that our present situation is due to *inadequate attention on the part of the Chil- dren's Aid Society* or discrimination against the placement of children with us ... Part of the troubles are no doubt due *to the closing, in so far as boys are concerned, of the Protestant Orphans' Home in 1943 and the Ladies Benevolent Society in 1947*. These to a degree were feeder institutions ... and no serious attempt has been made ... to offset this loss" (Weredale House Archives, 7 November 1950). A letter from the Weredale House board of governors to the Montreal Council of Social Agencies com- mittee set up to mediate between Weredale House and the Children's Aid Society observes: "in the past three years, during which we have suffered a drastic reduction in the numbers of children coming to us from the Children's Aid Society, the Family Welfare Association shows a slight increase in the number of families under care ... the Protestant Foster Home Centre shows an increase of 11% in the number of days' care given to children and the Children's Aid Society shows an 18% increase in the number of applications ... we are convinced that certain

of the Executive Workers of the Children's Aid Society do not believe in our type of care for children and, under these circumstances, our Institution has little possibility of being properly supplied" (Weredale House Archives, correspondence on the question of intake, 1 December 1950).

23 The resolution passed on 31 May 1950 and repeated in subsequent correspondence concluded: "Should we make direct contact with the Provincial Department of Welfare and Youth to qualify wherever possible for the acceptance of the care of dependent and neglected children?" A meeting of the Children's Aid Society board of directors also notes that "Weredale House had asked certain specific questions, such as whether it should do its own intake or at least accept referrals from other agencies, and whether or not it should seek to become a Youth Protection School. In other words, there was clear indication that Weredale House desired major changes in the relation of the agencies" (Weredale House Archives, correspondence on the question of intake, 13 December 1950).

24 The Children's Aid Society's board of directors, worrying that "Weredale House had gone so far as to suggest a possible change in the functions of the Children's Aid Society to include the active discovery of some children who needed care," observed that there was "an important need for agencies to work together towards a common end and show a united front, particularly in relation to the Provincial Government, so that the government in extending its interests would not be confused by several agencies presenting varied ideas" (Weredale House Archives, correspondence on the question of intake, 13 December 1950).

25 Summerhill House (for girls) does not seem to have considered becoming a youth-protection school and did not renegotiate its arrangement with the Children's Service Centre. As the result of declining referrals from this source during the 1950s, the institution shut down in 1961. In 1964, against the recommendation of external child-welfare experts (who suggested affiliation with the Children's Service Centre as a foster-home placement agency), its board of directors chose to reopen Summerhill House, on a small scale, as group homes for girls.

26 The only other Protestant youth-protection school was the Girls' Cottage School, the reform school for anglophone girls.

27 Private children's institutions had little financial incentive to become youth-protection schools, because they already received public funding through the Quebec Public Charities Act.

CHAPTER FOUR

1 Allancroft was established as an emergency shelter and a residential observation centre in a Montreal suburb. It gave "the appearance of a

small farmstead, set well back on a spacious open lot"; it cared for up to fourteen children at a time (between the ages of five and fourteen) in a "warm and homelike atmosphere"; and children attended school on the premises. Staffed by non-professional housemothers, Allancroft housed children whose current and future placements were determined by caseworkers from the Children's Service Centre (Chan et al 1957).

2 Although a majority of the children were discharged successfully from Allancroft to foster homes (in the sense that their placement lasted at least six months), "three-fourths of the total breakdowns in foster homes were caused by situational factors" that included abusive foster parents, interference from the child's own parents, and illness in the foster family (Chan et al 1957, 172).

3 There was a shift from a predominance of children in the five- to eight-year-old age range to children in the nine- to eleven-year-old age range.

4 Roughly half the children stayed at Allancroft for less than three months.

5 Public funding provided free hospital care but not free medical care of the more general kind until 1968. As a result, the hospital-insurance legislation "opened the floodgates of consumer demand for hospital care" and led to "a spectacular increase in the number of hospital beds, to spiralling costs, and to an increased emphasis ... on a type of health care directly related to hospitalization" (Lesemann 1984, 82). For a thorough analysis of changes in the health sector in the Province of Quebec, particularly of those leading up to its transformation in 1970, see Renaud (1976).

6 It is also our impression, from reading clinical descriptions of clients at the Douglas Hospital's adolescent psychiatric wing, that hospitals selected emotionally disturbed clients whose behaviour was passive rather than aggressive. If so, aggressively disturbed youth must have been sent elsewhere. A similar preference was noted by Teram in his observations of the later period, covered in Part Three. But it is also worth noting that client-selection practices at research-oriented institutions like the Douglas Hospital (see Shamsie 1967) may also have been shaped to some extent by ongoing research agendas.

7 The Mental Hygiene Institute was established in 1919, as the result of a survey of children in Montreal's Protestant schools, by the Canadian National Committee for Mental Hygiene. It became a member of the Montreal Council of Social Agencies in 1923. As a medical and psychiatric outpatient clinic, the Mental Hygiene Institute diagnosed and treated children referred by Montreal's Protestant child-welfare organizations – for psychological testing and evaluation prior to adoption (one-third of all referrals), "conduct disorders, personality problems,

vocational guidance, school failure, mental defect and mental disease" (Thompson 1950, 97; see also Mayotte 1949).

8 The "experiment" evaluated the effectiveness of the drug in an applied clinical, rather than a scientific, way. Although there were "control" and "experimental" groups, the dosages for boys in the experimental group were adjusted individually, on the basis of informally structured behaviour reports from cottage parents. These "parents" were aware of the membership, and changing dosages, of the boys in both groups.

9 In 1957, responsibility for children's institutions (funded under the Public Charities Act) was transferred from the Department of Health to the Department of Social Welfare and Youth, thus consolidating provincial responsibility for youth protection schools and children's institutions into one department.

10 By including Brother Jacques on the survey team the survey also created new contacts with Montreal's francophone youth protection schools; Brother Jacques was familiar with procedures at Mont St-Antoine, the traditional reform school for boys, and at Boscoville, the model treatment-oriented institution created in 1954. Provincial support for The Boys' Farm in the late 1960s was facilitated by Boscoville's reputation in the francophone sector as a showcase facility.

11 A letter written by a boy at The Boys' Farm to his mother on 28 January 1966 pleads: "So help me God, this God-damned *Hell* is literally driving me out of my mind! It has come to the point that I refuse to go downstairs (in the basement) unless a supervisor is down there! Yesterday, when the cottage parent was not around, I was cornered in a hole and punched and kicked by *TWELVE GUYS* out of the 15 in the cottage – and that isn't the first time it has happened!" Victor Malarek's account of life at Weredale House during the early 1960s provides a similar description of life for boys there, including the use of nonsupervised basements for fights (Malarek 1984).

12 Material concerning the Child and Family Clinic comes, in part, from Douglas Hospital annual reports for 1965–71 (Douglas Hospital).

13 A court-assessment clinic for francophone children had existed since 1945, but lacked anglophone personnel.

14 The institutions for boys included Weredale House, Summerhill Homes (which planned to open two group homes for boys), and The Boys' Farm.

15 In 1966, the Child and Family Clinic estimated that about 28 per cent of the children appearing before the Montreal Social Welfare Court could be classified as English-speaking, and that 25 per cent of these were referred to the clinic for assessment.

16 The Youth Protection Schools Act specified that the mental or physical inadmissibility of a child "shall be determined by the clinical services

designated by the Minister." The judges argued that the Child and Family Clinic constituted this clinical service.

17 The Child and Family Clinic put many boys on probation: "The figures available at the Child and Family Clinic at the Social Welfare Court indicate that in 1966, out of 285 boys who were screened, 24 were admitted at the Boys' Farm and 180 returned to their homes on probation" (BFTS, reports, Shamsie report, April 1967, 5).

18 The president of The Boys' Farm summarized the situation as he had presented it to the deputy minister of Family and Social Welfare: "I put us on record very clearly, stating that: 1) our population was at a long term low; 2) we were running behind $8,000 a month; 3) this could clean us out of the last of any resources we had in one year, apart from any provision for our current $50,000 overdraft; 4) that there was no question ... of our increasing our private incomes through a campaign, because under present circumstances we felt we had nothing to sell" (BFTS, internal correspondence, 29 September 1966).

19 The Children's Service Centre (Protestant), the Catholic Welfare Bureau, and the Baron de Hirsch Institute (Jewish) launched the Foster Home Recruiting Centre.

20 In contrast to Weredale House, Summerhill Homes was, however, a "respecialized institution" at this time; its original institution for girls had been depopulated by foster-home placement, and its two small group homes filled with disturbed girls referred from psychiatric wards. This may reflect differences in how girls were treated. Because they were fewer in number, they may have been easier to place for adoption or in foster homes.

21 Weredale House refused delinquent boys, and the fact that its clients attended the local community school discouraged the referral of boys whose educational needs or degree of emotional disturbance made normal school attendance impossible. From the point of view of child-welfare experts, Weredale was therefore an "over-used" institution.

22 In spite of its lavish endowment, Summerhill's board of directors was concerned about the relatively high costs per child of group-home care, compared with the institutional care it had previously provided. The ambiguous status of group homes affected provincial financial support: although the province agreed to provide support for twelve children at the $5.00 per diem rate for institutions, additional children were supported at the $2.20 per diem foster-care rate. These financial considerations not only limited expansion for a time, but also appear to have acted as a source of contention between Summerhill's traditionally oriented board and its new activist executive director – a professional social worker.

23 Summerhill Homes established two group homes in 1964, and a third in 1965. They were located separately in middle-class neighborhoods,

staffed by houseparents (husband and wife, with their own children) and supported by professional casework staff from the agency. The group homes were intended to provide "intensive casework therapy" in a "family-oriented milieu." Each group home housed about nine clients who attended local schools.

24 Summerhill was, nevertheless, a comparatively small institution. Between 1964 and 1967, it housed thirty-seven children, primarily girls. Weredale House had average annual populations of over 150 during these years.

25 The president of Summerhill's board of directors wrote to the president of Weredale's board, "Before we make a decision on this move, we want to acquaint your Board with this plan and ask for your advice, since Weredale House has cared for boys of this age for so many years. In your opinion, are there boys who could profit more from living in a small group home? Can you see any conflict between such a program and the type of care offered by Weredale House? Would you like to discuss this matter in more detail with us, perhaps in a meeting between the Presidents and the Executive Directors of the two agencies?" (Summerhill Homes Archives, NA, MG 28, I, 405, vol. 6, file 19, 10 November 1966).

26 The serious population drop at The Boys' Farm in 1966 illustrates some of the difficulties in interpreting statistics – as historical studies must often do – without other sources of information. Without knowing more about the struggle between the reform school and the court over older delinquents and disturbed protection cases (from internal documents), and without being able to see how clients were redirected to the penitentiary and detention center (from internal documents or a broader set of institutional statistics), this drop would look like the successful decarceration of youth.

CHAPTER FIVE

1 The refusal of the Duplessis administration to participate in new federal hospitalization and unemployment insurance (public assistance) programs in 1957 helped to elect Jean Lesage's Liberals on a strong reformist platform in 1960 (Renaud 1976, 61–2; Lesemann 1987, 355).

2 "The new ideal of French-Canadian nationalists became a highly efficient technological society led by French Canadians and animated by a French spirit. The consuming goal of French-Canadian nationalists became *rattrapage*, catching up to social and economic development ... the lag in political modernization was most evident in the areas of education, health, and welfare. Here the Quebec provincial government had allowed private institutions – primarily those of the Church – to

retain a much greater degree of power and authority than was the case in the other provinces. It was in this same area that there occurred the most impressive expansion of governmental activities during the Lesage regime" (McRoberts 1988, 129, 131).

3 In 1961, the newly established Department of Family and Social Welfare appointed a committee to study the rising costs of public assistance and "certain problems arising particularly from the application of the Quebec Public Charities Act" (Quebec 1963, 9). The Study Committee on Public Assistance issued its report – known as the Boucher report – in 1963 (see Quebec 1963).

4 The Boucher report proposed a 'partnership' between the public and private sectors, in which provincial government funds and coordinative control would transform private social welfare organizations into "para-public" ones. "*Para-public* is a term used in Quebec to describe voluntary agencies working in close collaboration with governmental agencies and generally receiving their major financial support from public funds, while continuing to be managed by autonomous voluntary boards of directors." (National Study Service 1967a, 40)

5 As a result: "Beginning in the mid-1960s, using the additional funds it had won in its struggle with the federal government, it began to reform significantly the system of delivering social service. Gradually the church was relieved of its responsibility for hospitals and other social services such as orphanages and asylums. These were integrated into a single system under the control of the provincial government" (Coleman 1984, 138).

6 "By the early 1970s Ontario and New Brunswick were the only two provinces not to receive funds under the Canada Assistance Plan as they refused to transfer juvenile-correctional services to welfare agencies" (Osborne 1979, 21).

7 Montreal's private Protestant child welfare organizations reported increasing deficits from 1957 through 1965. The resulting cutbacks in service led the Montreal Council of Social Agencies to refer to 1965 as the "year of retrenchment" (Montreal Council of Social Agencies, *Red Feather Year Book*, 1965).

8 These were the Family Service Association, the Society for the Protection of Women and Children, and the Children's Service Centre.

9 Minutes from these meetings can be found in the Weredale House Archives, NA, MG 28, I 405, vol. 8, file 5 (Survey of Red Feather Child and Family Services sponsored by the Montreal Council of Social Agencies – Correspondence, reports and memorandum, 1966–67).

10 At the first meeting on 24 March 1966, several agency representatives spoke against the proposal, making "repeated references" to the

"considerable animosity" created by the surveys carried out in 1924 and 1935.

11 At the 24 March 1966 meeting, a Montreal Council of Social Agencies official was reported as stating that "other parts of the province are apprehensive about the government taking over and he felt that we should be looking ahead and thinking about future priorities and opportunities for service"; at the 3 May 1966 meeting, he again stressed that "he felt that we had now come to the turning point in the road and that one of the basic issues was the division of long-term responsibility and deciding what should be assumed by the government and what should be assumed by private agencies."

12 These included the anglophone Federation of Catholic Charities, and the Conseil des oeuvres de Montréal, the federation of francophone welfare organizations. The threat of provincial intervention thus also produced new contacts across the sectarian and language lines that had divided Montreal's social welfare federations.

13 The National Study Service, an American consulting group composed of child welfare experts, was familiar with the Montreal situation, having just completed a similar survey for the anglophone Federation of Catholic Charities.

14 As the executive director of one children's institution observed, "The province was not going to wait much longer for us to put our house in order according to what they were saying publicly and privately" (Weredale House Archives, Montreal Council of Social Agencies meeting, 24 March 1966).

15 The impact of the Caplan-Marcilio criticisms on the Child and Family Clinic and court commitments was discussed in a meeting of the administration committe of The Boys' Farm on 11 October 1966. Dr Shamsie was engaged and began his work in November 1966.

16 In January 1967, the board of directors planned to submit recommendations from the Shamsie report as its brief to the Castonguay commission.

17 Richard Clendenen was a law professor at the University of Minnesota who had held previous teaching and administrative positions in social work and child welfare.

18 The Boys' Farm arranged for Dr Shamsie and Professor Clendenen to meet, thus ensuring input from their own local expert into the National Study Service survey.

19 The board president announced the new policies in a letter addressed to the deputy minister of the Department of Family and Social Welfare on 7 July 1967; copies of the letter were sent to other provincial officials with whom The Boys' Farm dealt in Montreal. The letter read, "You

will be glad to know we are in the process of refitting McCall Cottage which, as a place of close confinement with a capacity of about 20 boys, will serve as an interim measure in our adoption of a new policy to maintain an area of close confinement within our open institution." (BFTS, external correspondence, 21 June 1967)

20 The board announced, "We are accordingly looking for a clinical director with an M.S.W. degree to install programmes under adequate trained personnel" on 7 July 1967. In November, Ronald Wylie began work as director of services.

21 These nine subtypes were: asocial aggressive, asocial passive, immature conformist, cultural conformist, manipulator, neurotic anxious, neurotic acting-out, cultural identifier, and situational emotional reactor. See Warren (1969) for a more complete presentation of this classification scheme and its use in the California Community Treatment Project, launched in 1961. (For a later evaluation of the net widening impact of the CCTP, see Lerman 1975.)

22 Provincial officials, intending to modernize Quebec's child-welfare system, were highly attuned to the advice of child-welfare experts. The Department of Family and Social Welfare not only provided partial support for the external surveys, but were also influenced by the results. In 1968, the department's director of institutional resources in Montreal emphasized his strong support for The Boys' Farm's new plans and budget requests, but advised Wylie that the department's financial services section "definitely wanted to know whether or not our (The Boys' Farm's) consultants backed the new program" (BFTS, board minutes, 27 November 1968).

23 The number of court-referred admissions to Weredale House increased from ten in 1966 to twenty-seven in 1967; after 1967, they accounted for about a third of all admissions. (Weredale House Archives, NA, MG 28, I 405, vol. 1, file 5; statistics from minutes of annual meetings used in annual reports, 1922–71).

24 The number of clients discharged by Weredale House to the court and other agencies rose from twelve in 1967, to twenty-eight in 1968–69, and to fifty-one in 1969–70. Between 1968 and 1971, these clients accounted for between 29 and 48 per cent of all discharged clients (Weredale House Archives, NA, MG 28, I 405, vol. 1, file 5).

25 In its annual report for 1966, the Children's Service Centre, which ran this small institution for "deeply disturbed boys and girls," reported that "pressure increased from the Social Welfare Court (and) the Montreal Children's Hospital ... to accept children because of their physical or emotional problems" (Montreal Council of Social Agencies, *Red Feather Year Book*, 1966, 45).

26 In 1966, Dr Marcilio reported that boys sent to The Boys' Farm had spent from three weeks to six months in the detention centre.

27 Youth protection schools used the detention center to hold difficult clients, particularly runaways. The letter notified them not to send more clients to the detention centre, and to take back the clients they had sent. This re-routed some difficult clients to Centre Berthelet, the locked juvenile facility that began operation in 1964.

28 The Group Care Committee included the provincial Department of Family and Social Welfare's director of institutional resources and representatives from Montreal's anglophone children's institutions.

29 The National Study Service (1967b, 27) reported that Summerhill's clients were "difficult and disturbed ... many have histories of hospitalization, delinquencies or multiple replacements in foster care."

30 Summerhill Homes Archives, NA, MG 28, I 388, vol. 18, file 17: Psychiatric Services at the Jewish General Hospital, 1966–71.

31 These discussions are reported in meetings of the board of governors of The Boys' Home (Weredale House) on 20 February 1969, 15 October 1969, 11 November 1969, 9 December 1969, 18 January 1970, and 15 February 1971 (Weredale House Archives, NA, MG 28, I 405, vol. 6, file 4). Also see the Batshaw report (Quebec 1976, 998).

32 The letter is quoted at length in the minutes of the 15 February 1971 meeting of the Board of Governors of The Boys' Home (Weredale House, Ibid.).

33 The Child and Family Clinic was phased out in 1973. Its functions were turned over to the regional social-service centres created in 1971 – and therefore to the child-welfare professionals who staffed these centres.

PART THREE: INTRODUCTION

1 Each region has a council which in turn has an administrative committee. These two groups act as both the planning and monitoring bodies for health and social services in their region.

2 The act specifies interrelated responsibilities and the membership of interlocking boards of directors.

3 The Batshaw committee report (Quebec 1976) provided a grim and detailed picture of institutions for "socially disturbed" children in the province.

4 The joint-admissions committee therefore represents the director of youth protection's decision to delegate authority to the committee and to intervene only in urgent cases or in cases of unresolvable conflict.

5 Juvenile courts became known as social welfare courts after 1950, and as youth courts after 1977.

6 There is an additional, smaller, social service centre – the Jewish Family Services Social Service Centre – serving the anglophone Jewish community. The larger social service centre that we observed – the Ville Marie Social Services Centre – is the second-largest such centre in the province. Montreal's francophone social service centre – the Centre de services sociaux du Montréal métropolitain – is the largest.

7 The social service centre included a resource development division with social workers working in hospitals, schools, and reception centres, and dealt with issues that could not be divided geographically.

8 Youth Horizons merged Weredale House, Summerhill House, Allancroft Observation Centre, and the Girls' Cottage School.

9 There are three additional, small reception centers in the network. One, Mount Saint Patrick, competes with Youth Horizons for preadolescents (under the age of twelve) with behavioural and emotional problems.

10 This policy was made possible by contradictions between the provincial Act Respecting Health and Social Services (1971) and the later provincial Youth Protection Act (1977). The first act gave reception centres the right to define their admissions criteria (a court order, in this case) and to refuse clients who do not meet them. The second act, however, allows the director of youth protection to place youth in reception centres on a "voluntary measures" basis – that is, without going to court. This policy will be discussed further.

CHAPTER SIX

1 Referrals to psychiatric programs could also be made through direct application or referral (including referrals from the social service centre). The joint-admissions committee did not, therefore, process all referrals to psychiatric programs for adolescents. It did, however, process all placements in reception centres, including placements in reception-centre day programs.

2 The centralized committee also reviewed the few referrals of anglophone clients from outside Montreal, and from Montreal's Jewish Family Services Social Service Center.

3 Reception centres nevertheless developed their own network of foster homes in which they placed youths as they progressed through the reception centres' continuum of programs.

4 "Escalation" is a term used by professionals and clients alike within the youth-protection network.

5 In a couple of cases, one psychiatrist agreed to accept clients for assessment and then transfer them to Youth Horizons. This cooperation was possible because of the interpersonal trust between the two

institutional representatives involved and the dissimilarity of the programs they represented.

6 Unless otherwise stated, the quoted material, and other observations reported in Part Three of this book, come from the field work and interviews carried out by Eli Teram. The sites and methods used to make and record these observations are described in the Appendix. More detailed field notes and identification of sources can be found in Teram 1986.

7 Reception centres had long waiting lists. The committee's decision not to refuse this client (and his worker) put him on a waiting list. The committee's decisions both to accept and to refuse referrals therefore affected the length of waiting lists.

8 Our discussion of the "director of youth protection" in this book glosses over the fact that some of the actions attributed to the person occupying this position were actually performed by his subordinates, called "review analysts" because they dealt with the periodic reviews written by delegates. In practice, workers and managers used the shorthand expression "DYP" when talking either about the director of youth protection himself, or the subordinates who exercised his authority. Since they made no distinction between the director of youth protection and his subordinates, this analysis mixes the two as well.

CHAPTER SEVEN

1 A fourth committee dealt with referrals from schools, hospitals, and other community resources not affiliated with the area service centres. Teram's observations did not include this committee.

2 This process of rationalizing escalated placement decisions is described in more detail in Teram (1988b).

3 For a more detailed account of the processes of restructuring the admissions committee, see Teram (1988a).

4 As students, adolescents are sent to and released from institutions in cycles that correspond to the school year. This occurs for two reasons. First, schools also engage in the selection of "good clients" and send troublesome or truant youths elsewhere, thus expanding institutional populations during the school year. Second, institutional stays are geared to the school year (whether clients attend school within the institution or at local schools), thus releasing more clients at the beginning of summer.

5 This control was also exercised less directly because the recentralized committee operated within the regional resource development division rather than under the director of youth protection. Review analysts

from the department of youth protection continued to sit on the area service-centre placement committees.

CHAPTER EIGHT

1 For comparison between the review of institutional placements in Quebec and Ontario, see Teram and Erickson (1988).

2 They were participants in a conference, entitled "Bill 24: One year after, 1980," that focused on Quebec's child-welfare system after the introduction of the Youth Protection Act.

3 Psychiatric hospitals also tried to maintain their traditional control over admissions. When the director of youth protection tried to enforce his placement authority by directly ordering a client into a psychiatric hospital, the hospital responded by freezing admissions pending review of their admissions policy.

4 To diffuse the potential conflict regarding this issue, Shawbridge called these workers "social service practitioners" and Shawbridge representatives consistently corrected any reference to these workers as "social workers." This game of titles in fact became an on-going joke in some meetings.

5 These two small social service centres, the Jewish Family Services Social Services Center serving Montreal's Jewish community and the other serving the anglophone community outside Montreal, placed youths in the anglophone reception centres, but not in sufficient numbers to warrant membership on the joint-admissions committees discussed in chapters 6 and 7.

6 These social workers were contracted through the Regional Resource Development Division.

7 The proposed policy would have assigned clients to social workers as clients arrived, sending social workers to various units to deal with clients. The current policy assigned clients to workers on a program basis, so that social workers remained involved with clients and the teams in the same one or two units.

8 Supervisors had their own reasons for managing conflicts without involving the director of youth protection, one being to enhance their own power. These dynamics are described in Teram (1986) and Teram and Erickson (1988).

9 The perception of both the legitimacy and the sanctions associated with role expectations have been used to predict conflict resolution activities (Gross et al 1964).

10 Taylor and Bogdan (1979) report a similar practice on the part of directors of institutions for the mentally handicapped.

CHAPTER NINE

1 J. Bagnall, "Judge Specifies Institution Where Boy Must Be Placed,"
Montreal Gazette, 1 February 1989.

APPENDIX

1 I was led to a small portion of this material by a letter from a public
   relations consultant at Shawbridge Youth Centres looking for "a student,
   perhaps a history student, who would be interested in writing the history of this Agency as a thesis project" (Aksich 1981). The letter was
   addressed to Dr Stanley Frost, head of the History of McGill Project,
   on the grounds that "many of the same great names from McGill's past
   were very active in the growth and development of this Agency."
      The letter mentioned "binders with newspaper clippings in chrono-
   logical order (relatively so) from 1917, and minute books from 1907."
   These materials were kept at the Montreal headquarters of Shawbridge
   Youth Centres probably because they *looked* old and interesting. I discovered the bulk of the material when I asked permission to look into
   the two attics of the administration building at Shawbridge's original
   Boys' Farm site.
2 See the references for Weredale House and Summerhill Homes for more
   information regarding these materials and access to them.
3 Although these archives were useful and a great deal easier to examine
   than The Boys' Farm attic material, the material was strikingly less voluminous and less candid. It is hard to tell whether this reflects the
   habits of those who kept the records, those who stored them (or threw
   them out), or those who selected them for presentation to the National
   Archives.
4 Montreal Council of Social Agency material is listed in the Bibliography.
5 Youth Horizons and Shawbridge Youth Centres permitted me to attend
   their meetings, but Mount Saint Patrick considered the meetings too
   sensitive and politely declined my request to attend.

Bibliography

Aikin, D. 1950. "The Role of the Montreal Council of Social Agencies in the establishment of Public Assistance." Master's thesis, School of Social Service Administration, University of Chicago.

Aksich, K. O. 1981. Letter addressed to Dr Stanley Brice Frost, 19 June.

Allison, S., and L. Prosser. 1983. *Montreal: English Language Social Services 1788–1982* (Chart). Montreal: Alliance Quebec.

Austin, J., and B. Krisberg. 1981. "Wider, Stronger, and Different Nets: The Dialectics of Criminal Justice Reform." *Journal of Research in Crime and Delinquency* 18 (1): 165–96.

Bala, N. 1988. "The Young Offenders Act: A Legal Framework." In *Justice and the Young Offenders Act*, edited by J. Hudson, J.P. Hornick and B.A. Burrows, 11–35. Toronto: Wall & Thompson.

Becker, H.S., and B. Geer. 1957. "Participant Observation and Interviewing: A Comparison." *Human Organization* 16 (3): 28–32.

Behiels, M.D. 1985. *Prelude to Quebec's Quiet Revolution*. Montreal: McGill-Queen's.

Benson, K.J. 1977. "Organizations: a Dialectical View." *Administrative Science Quarterly* 22: 1–21.

Blau, P.M., and W.R. Scott. 1962. *Formal Organizations*. San Francisco: Chandler.

Bortner, M.A. 1986. "Traditional Rhetoric, Organizational Realities: Remand of Juveniles to Adult Court." *Crime and Delinquency* 32 (1): 53–73.

Boys' Home (Montreal). *see* Weredale House

Boys' Farm and Training School (BFTS). Available at Shawbridge Youth Centres, 9000 L'Acadie, Montreal, Quebec, Canada H4N 2Y8.

– Annual reports for most years, 1907–50.

– External correspondence.

– Internal correspondence.

– Minutes of administration committee, 1929–50.

– Minutes of the meetings of board of directors, 1907–50.
– Reports, including the Caplan report (1966), the Marcilio report (1966), the Shamsie Survey (1966) and the Shamsie Report (1967)
– Scrapbooks of newspaper clippings, 1920–50.
Caldwell, G. 1967. "Boys' Home of Montreal – Weredale House." National Study Service Report. Weredale House Archives NA MG 28, I 405, vol 8, file 12.
Canada. 1908. The Juvenile Delinquents Act, *Statutes of Canada*, 7–8 ed. 7, 1908, c.40.
– 1921. House of Commons. *Debates*, 1921 Session, 1069, 3319.
– 1927. The Prisons and Reformatories Act, *Revised Statutes of Canada*, c. 163, and *Revised Statutes of Canada*, 1952, c. 217.
– 1929. The Juvenile Delinquents Act, *Revised Statutes of Canada*, 19–20 George V, 1929, c. 160.
– 1938. *Report of the Royal Commission to Investigate the Penal System of Canada* (Archambault report). Ottawa: J.O. Patenaude.
– 1965. *Juvenile Delinquency in Canada*. Report of the Department of Justice Committee on Juvenile Delinquency. Ottawa: Roger Duhamel.
– 1982. Young Offenders Act. *Revised Statutes of Canada*, c. 20.
Canadian Welfare Council. 1942. *Juvenile Courts in Canada*. Ottawa: Canadian Welfare Council, Pub. no. 121.
Caputo, T., and D.C. Bracken. 1988. "Custodial Dispositions and the Young Offenders Act." In *Justice and the Young Offenders Act*, edited by J. Hudson, J.P. Hornick and B.A. Burrows, 123–43. Toronto: Wall & Thompson.
Chan, M., G. Greenblatt, L. McDonald, F. Shulman, D. Thompson and A. Wyllie. 1957. "A Study of Allancroft, a Children's Institution." Master's thesis, School of Social Work, McGill University.
The Citizen (Montreal). 1922. "Farm Solves Boy Problem; Salvages Citizens." 28 October.
Clendenen, R., 1967a. "Boys' Farm and Training School, Shawbridge, Quebec." *National Study Service Report*. Montreal: Montreal Council of Social Agencies and Boys' Farm and Training School.
– 1967b. "Social Welfare Court, Probation Services and Detention Care." *National Study Service Report*. Quebec Government (1970), *La Societe face au crime* (Prevost Report): 659–68.
Cohen, S. 1979a. "Community Control – A New Utopia." *New Society* 29 (March 15): 609–11.
– 1979b. "The Punitive City: Notes on the Dispersal of Social Control." *Contemporary Crises* 3 (4): 339–63.
– 1985. *Visions of Social Control*. Cambridge: Polity Press.
Coleman, W.D. 1984. *The Independence Movement in Quebec 1945–1980*. Toronto: University of Toronto Press.
Copp, T. 1974. *The Anatomy of Poverty*. Toronto: McClelland and Stewart.

Crozier, M., and Thoenig, J.C. 1976. "The Regulation of Complex Organized Systems". *Administrative Science Quarterly* 21: 547–70.

Curran, D.J. 1988. "Destructuring, Privatization, and the Promise of Juvenile Diversion: Compromising Community-based Corrections." *Crime & Delinquency* 34 (4): 363–78.

Dawson, O. 1952. *"My Story of the Boys' Farm at Shawbridge."* Montreal. Available at McGill University and Concordia University libraries.

Doob, A. 1983. "Turning Decisions into Non-Decisions." In *Current Issues in Juvenile Justice*, eds. R. Corrado, M. LeBlanc and J. Trepanier. 147–89 Toronto: Butterworths.

Douglas Hospital. 1965–1973. *Annual Reports.* Verdun: Douglas Hospital.

Douglas, J.D. 1976. *Investigative Social Research.* Beverly Hills, Calif.: Sage.

Douglas, M.H. 1967. "A History of the Society for the Protection of Women and Children in Montreal." Master's thesis, School of Social Work, McGill University.

Emerson, R.M. 1969. *Judging Delinquents.* Chicago: Aldine.

Fombrun, C.J. 1986. "Structural Dynamics within and between Organizations." *Administrative Science Quarterly* 31: 403–21.

Foucault, M. 1977. *Discipline and Punish.* New York: Random House.

Gazette (Montreal). 1922. "Juvenile Court Cases Decrease." 4 January.

– 1924. "C.P.R. President Spoke on Underprivileged Boy." 6 April.

Girls' Cottage School Archives. NA, MG 28, I 404, Finding aid no. 1500.

Gross, N., W.S. Mason, and A.W. McEachern. 1958. *Explorations in Role Analysis: Studies of the School Superintendency Role.* New York: Wiley.

Guarino-Ghezzi, S., and J.M. Byrne. 1989. "Developing a Model of Structured Decision Making in Juvenile Corrections: The Massachusetts Experience." *Crime and Delinquency* 35: 270–302.

Hackler, J. 1983. "The Challenge of Legislating Juvenile Justice: A Commentary on the Report of the Charbonneau Commission. Quebec." *Canadian Journal of Criminology* 25 (July): 354–60.

– 1983–84. "Interpreting Meaning in Juvenile Court: The Use of Local Wisdom. *Juvenile and Family Court Journal* 34 (4): 71–82.

– 1987. "In My Opinion ... The Impact of the Young Offenders Act." *Canadian Journal of Criminology* 29 (2): 205–9.

Hagan, J., and J. Leon. 1977. "Rediscovering Delinquency: Social History, Political Ideology, and the Sociology of Law," *American Sociological Review* 42(4): 587–98.

Harevan, T.K. 1969. "An Ambiguous Alliance: Some Aspects of American Influences on Canadian Social Welfare." *Histoire Sociale/Social History* 3 (April): 82–100.

Hatch, A.J. 1987. "Treatment Orders and Mentally Disordered Young Offenders: Conflicting Philosophies and the Implementation of the Young Offenders Act." Paper presented at the American Society of Criminology meetings, Montreal.

Hawkins, R., and G. Tiedeman. 1975. *The Creation of Deviance: Interpersonal and Organizational Determinants*. Columbus, Ohio: Charles E. Merrill.

Houston, S.E. 1972. "Victorian Origins of Juvenile Delinquency: A Canadian Experience." *History of Education Quarterly*, 12:254–80.

– 1982. "The 'Waifs and Strays' of a Late Victorian City: Juvenile Delinquents in Toronto." In *Childhood and Family in Canadian History*, edited by J. Parr, 129–42. Toronto: McClelland and Stewart.

Hudson, J., J.P. Hornick, and B. Burrows, eds. 1988. *Justice and the Young Offender in Canada*. Toronto: Wall and Thompson.

Ignatieff, M. 1978. *A Just Measure of Pain: The Penitentiary in the Industrial Revolution 1750–1850*. New York: Pantheon.

– 1981. "State, Civil Society and Total Institution: A Critique of Recent Social Histories of Punishment." In *Crime and Justice: An Annual Review of Research*, vol. 3, edited by M. Tonry and N. Morris. Chicago: University of Chicago Press.

Johnston, W. 1985. "Keeping Children in School: The Response of the Montreal Catholic School Commission to the Depression of the 1930s." *Historical Papers/Communications Historiques*: 193–217.

Jones, A. 1978. "'Closing Penetanguishene Reformatory': An Attempt to Deinstitutionalize Treament of Juvenile Offenders in Early Twentieth Century Ontario." *Ontario History*. 70 (December): 227–44.

Kahn, R.L., D.M. Wolfe, R.P. Quinn, and J.D. Snoek. 1964. *Organizational Stress: Studies in Role Conflict and Ambiguity*. New York: John Wiley.

Katz, D., and R.L. Kahn. 1966. *The Social Psychology of Organizations*. New York: John Wiley.

Klein, M.W. 1979. "Deinstitutionalization and Diversion of Juvenile Offenders: A Litany of Impediments." In *Crime and Justice: An Annual Review of Research*, edited by N. Morris and M. Tonry, vol. 1: 145–201. Chicago: University of Chicago Press.

Krisberg, B., I.M. Schwartz, P. Litsky, and J. Austin. 1986. "The Watershed of Juvenile Justice Reform." *Crime and Delinquency* 32: 5–38.

Laflamme-Cusson, S., and M. Baril. 1975. *La detention des mineurs dans la region de Montreal* (4 vols.). Quebec: Ministère des Affaires Sociales.

Lang, C.L. 1981. "Good Cases—Bad Cases: Client Selection and Professional Prerogative in a Community Mental Health Center." *Urban Life*, 10 (3): 289–309.

LeBlanc, M., and H. Beaumont. 1988. "The Quebec Perspective on the Young Offenders Act: Implementation before Adoption." In *Justice and the Young Offender in Canada*, edited by J. Hudson, J.P. Hornick and B. Burrows, 81–92. Toronto: Wall and Thompson.

Lerman, P. 1975. *Community Treatment and Social Control: A Critical Analysis of Juvenile Correctional Policy*. Chicago: University of Chicago Press.

– 1982. *Deinstitutionalization and the Welfare State*. New Brunswick, N.J.: Rutgers University Press.

Leschied, A.W., and P.G. Jaffe. 1988. "Implementing the Young Offenders Act in Ontario." In *Justice and the Young Offender in Canada*, edited by J. Hudson, J.P. Hornick and B. Burrows, 65–79. Toronto: Wall and Thompson.

Lesemann, F. 1984. *Services and Circuses: Community and the Welfare State*. Montreal: Black Rose Books.

– 1987. "Social Welfare Policy in Quebec." In *Canadian Social Policy*, edited by S.A. Yelaja, 350–77. Waterloo, Ont.: Wilfrid Laurier University Press.

Lesemann, F., and G. Renaud. 1980. "Loi 24 et transformation des pratiques professionnelles en service social." *Intervention* 58 (summer): 25–57.

Lipsky, M. 1980. *Street-level Bureaucracy*. New York: Russell Sage Foundation.

McCleary, R. 1977. "How Parole Officers Use Records." *Social Problems* 24 (5): 576–89.

McDougall, D. 1985. "Children's Rights: An Evaluation of the Controversy." In *The Challenge of Child Welfare*, edited by K.L. Levitt and B. Wharf, 266–75. Vancouver: University of British Columbia Press.

MacGill, H.G. 1925. *The Juvenile Court in Canada*. Ottawa: Canadian Council on Child Welfare.

McRoberts, K. 1988. *Quebec: Social Change and Political Crisis*. 3d ed. Toronto: McClelland and Stewart.

Malarek, V. 1984. *Hey Malarek! The True Story of a Street Kid who Made It*. Toronto: Macmillan of Canada.

Markwart, A.A., and R. Corrado. 1989. "Is the Young Offenders Act More Punitive?" In *Young Offender Dispositions*, edited by L. Beaulieu, 7–26. Toronto: Wall and Thompson.

Mayotte, A.S. 1949. "Uses made of a Mental Hygiene Clinic by a Boys' Training School." Master's thesis, School of Social Work, McGill University.

Mendelsohn, L.E., and S. Ronald. 1969. "History of the Montreal Juvenile Court." Master's thesis, School of Social Work, McGill University.

Mennel, R.M. 1973. *Thorns and Thistles: Juvenile Delinquents in the United States 1825–1940*. Hanover, N.H.: University Press of New England.

– 1983. "Attitudes and Policies toward Juvenile Delinquency in the United States: A Historiographical Review." *Crime and Justice: An Annual Review of Research* 4: 191–224.

Messinger, S.L. 1978. "The Dumping Ground: Notes on the Evolution of a Prison." In *The Children of Ishmael*, edited by B. Krisberg and J. Austin, 392–409. Palo Alto, Calif.: Mayfield Publishing Co.

Meyer, J.W., and W.R. Scott. 1983. "Centralization and the Legitimacy Problems of Local Government." In *Organizational Environments: Ritual and Rationality*, edited by J.W. Meyer and W.R. Scott, 199–215. Beverly Hills, Calif.: Sage.

Mongeau, S. 1967. *Évolution de l'Assistance au Québec*. Montreal: Éditions du Jour.

Montreal Catholic Community Council. 1930. *Social Welfare Services of English Catholics*. Montreal: Montreal Catholic Community Council.

Montreal Council of Social Agencies (MCSA) also known as: (Welfare Federation, Red Feather). "Report of a Committee of the Montreal Council of Social Agencies" (Falk report). 1919. Montreal: MCSA. School of Social Work Library, McGill University, Montreal, Quebec.

– "A Study of the Children's Division of the Montreal Council of Social Agencies, made by the Child Welfare League of America" (Carstens report). 1924. Montreal: MCSA. Weredale House Archives NA MG 28, I 405.

– "Report of the Survey Committee." 1935. Eight sections, including "Report on Child Care and Protection (section two). School of Social Work Library, McGill University, Montreal, Quebec.

– *Red Feather Year Books*. 1958, 1962–67. Montreal: Welfare Federation of Montreal. McLennan-Redpath Library, McGill University, Montreal, Quebec.

– *Montreal and Metropolitan Region Survey on Psychiatric and Mental Health Services*. 1960. Prepared with Le Conseil des Oeuvres de Montréal. Montreal: Quebec Division Canadian Mental Health Association.

Montreal Star. 1922. "Less Crime Shown by Juvenile Court". 4 January.

– 1923a. "Less Liberty for Boys in U.S. Homes than Shawbridge: Visit to Training Institution on Hudson river by Owen Dawson." 7 July.

– 1923b. "Mrs. Fawns Swears Her Son Flogged by Welfare Workers." 12 October.

– 1924. "Juveniles' Judge Visits Boys' Farm." 22 November.

Moyer, S. 1980. *Diversion from the Juvenile Justice System and its Impact on Children: A Review of the Literature*. Ottawa: Minister of Supply and Services Canada.

National Study Service. 1967a. "Planning for Services to Families and Children in Greater Montreal." A National Study Service Report for the Montreal Council of Social Agencies. Weredale House Archives, NA, MG 28, I 405, vol. 8, file 15.

– 1967b. "Survey of Summerhill House." A National Study Service and Child Welfare League of America Report for Summerhill Homes in Montreal. Summerhill Homes Archives, NA MG 28, I 388, vol. 18, file 1.

– *See also* R. Clendenen, National Study Service Reports on The Boys' Farm and Training School and on the Montreal Social Welfare Court; and Caldwell, G. National Study Service Report on Weredale House.

Nearing, F.C. 1945. "A Study of The Boys' Farm and Training School at Shawbridge, Quebec." Master's thesis, School of Social Service, Université de Montréal.

Needleman, C. 1981. "Discrepant Assumptions in Empirical Research: The Case of Juvenile Court Screening." *Social Problems* 28 (3): 247–62.

Osborne, J.A. 1979. "Juvenile Justice Policy in Canada: The Transfer of the Initiative." *Canadian Journal of Family Law* 2: 7–32.

Peterson, R.D. 1988. "Youthful Offender Designations and Sentencing in the New York Criminal Courts." *Social Problems* 35: 111–30.

Peyrot, M. 1982. "Caseload Management: Choosing Suitable Clients in a Community Health Clinic Agency." *Social Problems* 30: 155–67.

Pfohl, S.J. 1978. *Predicting Dangerousness: The Social Construction of Psychiatric Reality*. Lexington, Mass: Lexington Books.

Platt, A. 1969. *The Child Savers*. Chicago: University of Chicago Press.

Polk, K. 1987. "When Less Means More: An Analysis of Destructuring in Criminal Justice." *Crime and Delinquency* 33 (2): 358–78.

Prottas, J. 1979. *People Processing*. Lexington, Mass: Lexington Books.

Pruger, R. 1973. "The Good Bureaucrat." *Social Work* 18 (4): 26–32.

Quebec, Government of 1910–49. *Sessional Papers*: Penal Establishments. Quebec: Proulx.

– 1910–67. *Statistical Yearbooks*: "Statistics of Reformatory Institutions" and "Statistics of Penal Institutions." Quebec: Proulx.

– 1910. An Act Respecting Juvenile Delinquents. *Statutes of Quebec*, 1 George V, 1910, c. 26.

– 1945. An Act to Constitute a Child Aid Clinic. *Statutes of Quebec*, 9 George VI, 1945, c. 25.

– 1950. An Act to Establish the Social Welfare Court. *Statutes of Quebec*, 14–15 George VI, 1950, c. 10.

– 1950. Youth Protection Schools Act. *Statutes of Quebec*, 8–9 Elizabeth II, c. 42.

– 1963. *Report of the Study Committee on Public Assistance* (Boucher report). Quebec: Government of Quebec.

– 1967–72. *Report of the Commission of Inquiry on Health and Social Welfare* (Castonguay-Nepveu report). Seven volumes including *Social Services 1972* (Part 4, tome 1). Quebec: Roch Lefebvre.

– 1970. *La Société face au crime*. Report of the Commission d'enquête sur l'administration de la justice en matière criminelle et pénale au Québec (Prevost report). Four volumes including *La cour de bien-être social* (vol. 4, tome 1) and *Étude comparative sur les tribunaux pour mineurs* (vol. 4, tome 3). Quebec: Roch Lefebvre.

– 1971. Act Respecting Health Services and Social Services. *Statutes of Quebec*, c. 48.

– 1976. *Rapport du Comité d'étude sur la réadaptation des enfants et adolescents placés en centre d'accueil* (Batshaw Report). Three volumes including the two volume *Guide des Centres D'Accueil de transition et de réadaptation du Québec*. Quebec: Direction des communications, Ministère des Affaires sociales.

- 1977. Youth Protection Act. *Statutes of Quebec*, c. 20.
- 1980. "Historique des affaires sociales au Québec". *Les Affaires Sociales au Québec*. Ministère des Affaires Sociales Québec: Imprimerie Boulanger, August.
- 1981. *Revised Regulations of Quebec*. S-5 R-2.
- 1982. *Rapport de la Commission Parlementaire spéciale sur la Protection de La Jeunesse* (Charbonneau report). Québec: Direction Générale des publications gouvernementales du Ministère des Communications.
- 1984. An Act to Amend the Youth Protection Act and other legislation. *Statutes of Quebec*, c. 4.

Rains, P. 1971. *Becoming an Unwed Mother*. Chicago: Aldine-Atherton.
- 1984. "Juvenile Justice and The Boys' Farm: Surviving a Court-Created Population Crisis, 1909–1948." *Social Problems* 31 (June): 500–13.
- 1985. "La Justice des mineurs et The Boys' Farm: 1909–1968." *Criminologie* 18 (1): 103–27.

Rains, P., and E. Teram. 1991. "The Transformation of Strategies for Controlling Admissions: Professionalization and Youth Processing Organizations." *Crime and Delinquency* 37 (2): 281–99.

Regnery, A.S. 1986. "A Federal Perspective on Juvenile Justice Reform." *Crime and Delinquency* 32: 39–51.

Renaud, M. 1976. "The Political Economy of the Quebec State Interventions in Health: Reform or Revolution?" Ph.D. dissertation, Sociology, University of Wisconsin (Madison).

Rooke, P.T., and R.L. Schnell. 1983. *Discarding the Asylum: From Child Rescue to the Welfare State in English Canada (1800–1950)*. Lanham, Md: University Press of America.

Rothman, C., and C. Scattolin. 1983. *Quebec Youth Law: The Youth Protection Act and the Young Offenders Act*. Montreal: Legal Information Research Group, McGill University.

Rothman, D.J. 1971. *Discovery of the Asylum: Social Order and Disorder in the New Republic*. Boston: Little, Brown.
- 1980. *Conscience and Convenience*. Boston: Little, Brown.

Rumilly, R. 1978. *Boscoville*. Montreal: Fides.

Schlossman, S.L. 1977. *Love and the American Delinquent*. Chicago: University of Chicago Press.

Scott, M.B., and S.M. Lyman. 1968. "Accounts." *American Sociological Review* 33: 46–62.

Scott, R.A. 1967a. "The Selection of Clients by Social Welfare Agencies: The Case of the Blind." *Social Problems* 14 (Winter): 248–57.
- 1967b. "The Factory as a Social Service Organization: Goal Displacement in Workshops for the Blind." *Social Problems* 15 (2): 160–75.

Scott, W.L. 1930. *The Juvenile Court in Law and the Juvenile Court in Action*. Ottawa: Canadian Council on Child Welfare.

Scull, A. 1977. *Decarceration*. Englewood Cliffs, N.J.: Prentice-Hall.

Shamsie, S.J. 1967. *Adolescent Psychiatry: Proceedings of a Conference Held at Douglas Hospital*. [Montreal]. "Published as a service to the medical profession by Schering Corporation Limited, Makers of Etrafon (brand of tranquilizer-antidepressant) and Trilafon (brand of perphenazine)."

Shawbridge Youth Centres. 1980. *The Social, Moral and Legal Obligation of Shawbridge vis-à-vis Bill 24.*

Shepherd, W.F. 1957. "The Genesis of the Montreal Council of Social Agencies." Master's thesis, School of Social Work, McGill University.

Statistics Canada. *Juvenile Delinquents*. Appearances before the court in the judicial district of Montreal (85–202), 1950–70.

– *Montreal: Population and housing characteristics by census tracts.* (95–404, 95–519, 95–704), 1951, 1961, 1970.

Summerhill Homes Archives. NA, MG 28, I 388, Finding aid no. 1504.

Sutherland, N. 1976. *Children in English-Canadian Society: Framing the Twentieth-Century Consensus*. Toronto: University of Toronto Press.

Taylor, S.J., and R. Bogdan. 1979. "Defending Illusions: Human Service Administrators in Organizations that Abuse People." Paper presented at the American Sociological Association, Boston, August 1979.

Teele, J.M., and S. Levine. 1968. "The Acceptance of Emotionally Disturbed Children by Psychiatric Agencies." In *Controlling Delinquents*, edited by S. Wheeler, 103–26. New York: John Wiley & Sons.

Teram, E. 1986. "The Interorganizational Processing of Clients and Information." Ph.D. dissertation, School of Social Work, McGill University.

– 1988a. "The Politics of Interorganizational Structures." *Canadian Social Work Review* 5 (Summer): 236–51.

– 1988b. "From Self-Managed Hearts to Collective Action: Dealing with Incompatible Demands in the Child Welfare System." *Children and Youth Services Review* 10: 305–15.

Teram, E., and G. Erickson. 1988. "The Protection of Children's Rights as Ceremony and Myth: A Critique of the Review of Institutional Placements in Quebec and Ontario." *Children and Youth Services Review* 10: 1–17.

Thompson, C.E.R. 1950. "Mental Health Services for Children in Quebec Province." Master's thesis, School of Social Work, McGill University.

Thompson, J. 1974. "Social Interdependence, the Polity and Public Administration." *Administration and Society* 6: 3–19.

Tremblay, P. 1984. "La punition charitable des délinquants juvéniles montréalais de 1859. à 1913." Montréal: Centre International de Criminologie, Université de Montréal.

Trepanier, J. 1983. "The Quebec Youth Protection Act: Institutionalized Diversion." In *Current Issues in Juvenile Justice*, edited by R. Corrado, M. LeBlanc and J. Trepanier, 191–202. Toronto: Butterworths.

– 1986. "La Justice des mineurs au Québec: 25 ans de transformations (1960–1985)." *Criminologie* 19 (1): 189–213.

– 1987. "Comment réagir à la délinquance juvénile: Les vues des parlementaires canadiens au début du siècle". Paper presented at Carleton University, colloque sur le droit canadien dans l'histoire, June.

Van Dusen, K.T. 1981. "Net Widening and Relabeling: Some Consequences of Deinstitutionalization." *American Behavioral Scientist* 24(6): 801–10.

Van Maanen, J. 1983. "Epilogue: Qualitative Methods Reclaimed". In *Qualitative Methodology*, edited by J. Van Maanen 247–68. Beverly Hills, Calif.: Sage.

Vigod, B.L. 1986. *Quebec before Duplessis: The Political Career of Louis-Alexandre Taschereau*. Montreal: McGill-Queen's.

– 1978. "Ideology and Institutions in Quebec. The Public Charities Controversy, 1921–1926." *Histoire sociale/Social History* 11 (21): 167–82.

– 1979. "The Quebec Government and Social Legislation During the 1930s: A Study in Political Self-destruction." *Journal of Canadian Studies* 14 (1): 59–69.

Warren, C.A.B. 1981. "New Forms of Social Control: The Myth of Deinstitutionalization." *American Behavioral Scientist* 24(6): 724–40.

Warren, C.A.B., and P. Guttridge. 1984. "Adolescent Psychiatric Hospitalization and Social Control." In *Mental Health and Criminal Justice*, edited by L.A. Teplin. Beverly Hills, Calif.: Sage.

Warren, M.Q. 1969. "The Case for Differential Treatment of Delinquents." *Annals of the American Academy of Political and Social Science* 38: 47–59.

Weredale House Archives. 1948–1970. Annual Reports and other materials. NA MG 28, I 405, Finding aid no. 1501.

West, W.G. 1984. *Young Offenders and the State*. Toronto: Butterworths.

Wilson, L.C. 1982. *Juvenile Courts in Canada*. Toronto: The Carswell Co.

Index

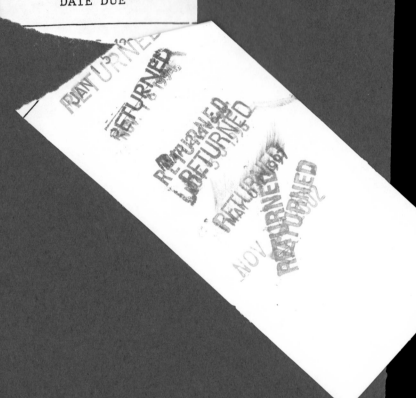